READING IN THE CONTENT AREAS
SOCIAL STUDIES 2

Laura Stark Johnson

PERMISSIONS

PATRICIA C. ACHESON for "The Checks and Balance System" from *Our Federal Government and How It Works*. Patricia C. Acheson. 4th edition. New York: Dodd, Mead & Co., 1984.

CHICAGO TRIBUNE COMPANY for "Back to the Land." © Copyrighted, Chicago Tribune Company, all rights reserved, used with permission.

for "Job, Life Quality Work Together." © Copyrighted, Chicago Tribune Company, all rights reserved, used with permission.

FACTS ON FILE, INC. for "Civil Rights." From *Key Issues in Constitutional History* edited by C. Carter Smith. Copyright © 1988 by Media Projects, Inc. Reprinted with permission of Facts On File, Inc., New York.

FRANKLIN WATTS for "The First New Deal" from *Franklin Delano Roosevelt: President of the People*. Roslyn and Ray Hiebert. New York: Franklin Watts, 1968.

LESLIE GERSON for "Getting More Smileage out of Your Life," from *A Lifetime of Health*, Northwestern Memorial Hospital, Chicago, July/August 1989.

ELLEN GRAY for "How Do Kids Really Feel about Being Home Alone?" originally published in *Children Today*, July–August 1987.

HARPER & ROW, PUBLISHERS, INC. for "The Jury System in America" from *Beyond a Reasonable Doubt* by Melvyn Zerman (Thomas Y. Crowell). Copyright © 1981 by Melvyn Zerman. Reprinted by permission of Harper & Row, Publishers, Inc.

HOUGHTON MIFFLIN COMPANY for excerpts from *The Water Is Wide* by Pat Conroy. Copyright © 1972 by Pat Conroy. Reprinted by permission of Houghton Mifflin Company.

LERNER PUBLICATIONS COMPANY for "Mexico" from *Mexico in Pictures,* copyright 1987 by Lerner Publications Company, 241 First Avenue North, Minneapolis, MN 55401. Used by permission of the publisher.

NEWSWEEK for "Cleaning up Our Mess." From *Newsweek*, July 24, 1989, © 1989, Newsweek, Inc. All rights reserved. Reprinted by permission.

for "What Happened to the Family?" From *Newsweek*, Winter/Spring Special Edition, © 1990, Newsweek, Inc. All rights reserved. Reprinted by permission.

ST. MARTIN'S PRESS, INC. for *North with the Spring* by Edwin Way Teale, Copyright © 1951, St. Martin's Press, Inc., New York.

SCHOLASTIC INC. for "The Evolution of One Person, One Vote" from *Update*, January 12, 1990, Copyright © 1990 by Scholastic Inc. Reprinted by permission.

for "Exploring the Global Village," "Canada: Struggling to Keep Its Identity," and "Nepal: Poverty amid Soaring Peaks," from *Update,* September 22, 1989, Copyright © 1989 by Scholastic Inc. Reprinted by permission.

U.S. DEPT. OF LABOR, BUREAU OF LABOR STATISTICS for information in "Labor Force Projections for the Year 2000," adapted from *Occupational Outlook Quarterly*, Fall 1989.

ISBN 0-88336-118-3

Copyright © 1991

 New Readers Press
Publishing Division of Laubach Literacy International
Box 131, Syracuse, New York 13210

Sponsoring Editor: Christina M. Jagger
Project Editor: Heidi Stephens
Graphic Artist: Mary Greenseich
Cover Design: Patricia Rapple
Cover Art: Stephen Rhodes
Reading Consultant: Randie Davidson Mosenthal

9 8 7 6 5 4 3 2

Table of Contents

Unit 1: Geography

the study of the earth's surface, climates, peoples, and natural resources

RIVER BLUFFS, 1,320 MILES ABOVE ST. LOUIS, 1832, George Catlin
National Museum of American Art, Washington, DC/Art Resource, NY

*Why is understanding different nations, peoples, and cultures
so important today? This selection shows the special resources and
problems two nations—Canada and Nepal—bring to the global village.*

The Bettmann Archive

EXPLORING THE GLOBAL VILLAGE

It seems silly to think of the Earth as made up of separate countries when we see it from space. From the perspective of the photo above, man-made borders blur and become insignificant compared to coastlines and clouds.

But back on Earth, we sometimes lose track of the fact that our world is bigger than the country in which we live. All too often we don't bother to look beyond our daily routines, let alone inquire into the lives of people in other parts of the planet.

"Why should I care about people in other countries?" you might ask. "How do they affect my life anyway?" Until the 20th century, that's the way many Americans felt. Isolated by the Atlantic and Pacific Oceans, the majority of Americans were content to ignore the rest of the world.

But today, thousands of satellites circle the globe, transmitting information around the world in an instant. Wars can be waged by remote control, wiping out entire populations at the touch of a button. Any country we choose to visit is only hours away by airplane. Today, one simple fact is inescapable—we are no longer simply citizens of a single country. We've become residents of what sociologists call a "global village." And in our increasingly interconnected world, our common future depends on understanding each other.

Canada: Struggling to Keep Its Identity

Adjacent to 13 American states, Canada is the United States' biggest and closest neighbor. Its southern edge runs 5,500 miles along the northern tier of the U.S.—the longest land border in the world.

That proximity has led to a strong alliance. The two sides have never been at war with each other, and each is the other's largest trading partner.

But despite its massive physical size—second only to the former Soviet Union's— Canada has always been North America's "other" country.

With deep-rooted ties to England and France and an ever-present American influence, Canadians have had to struggle to shape a national identity. Lately Canadians have worried that close relations with the U.S. are unraveling that fragile sense of self.

Their identity is fragile in part because the population is so spread out. A quarter of Canada's 26.3 million people— fewer than live in California—reside in rural areas and tend to cluster in lowlands near the U.S. border, away from the harsh arctic climate of the mountainous north.

In addition, most Canadian families hail from other countries. Canada's original inhabitants, the Native Americans, account for only two percent of the country's population; that includes the Inuit people, popularly known as Eskimos.

Two Languages

Forty percent of the people are of British ancestry, while 27 percent are descendants of the French. Both English and French are official languages. Official ceremonies—not to mention announcements at baseball and hockey games—are spoken in both tongues.

A sign in Canada gives directions in English and French, the nation's official languages.

The strong division between English-speaking and French-speaking inhabitants has caused problems in the country. The province[1] of Quebec, dominated by French Canadians, is home to a separatist movement[2] that seeks independent statehood.

Canadians are also divided over an agreement to become closer trading partners with the U.S. Many Canadians fear they will become a "51st state." The invasion of U.S. pop culture, for example, has led the government to require a "Canadian content quota" for broadcasting and publishing. In 1988, 95 percent of Canada's English-language programming came from America. The agreement eliminates many trade barriers, leading some to worry that U.S. companies will buy up Canadian firms.

The treaty was so controversial that Prime Minister Brian Mulroney was forced to call a general election before the legislation passed. Under the Canadian form of democracy, the Prime Minister cannot act without the approval of the House of Commons, the chief legislative body. If the House loses confidence in the leader, the Prime Minister must either resign or call a general election.

Mulroney succeeded in keeping the people's confidence and in passing the Free Trade Pact, but only by the narrowest of margins. The vote reflected the strong fear that Canadians will lose their national identity.

"Put plainly, we're paranoid,"[3] writes novelist Mordecai Richler. "French Canadians (are) fearful of being culturally overwhelmed by English Canadians, who are even more terrified of being swamped by the Americans."

---

1. **province:** one of the 10 main divisions of Canada
2. **separatist movement:** organized activities by people who favor breaking away from a group
3. **paranoid:** overly suspicious

Nepal: Poverty Amid Soaring Peaks

Perched on the mountainous border between India and China, the tiny nation of Nepal is often overshadowed by its better-known neighbors. But Nepal's strategic[4] location and its spectacular setting have long drawn travelers to one of the world's most exotic regions.

The Kingdom of Nepal packs an incredible range of culture and climate into a region only a little larger than Arkansas. Northern Nepal is the high peak region of the Himalayas. Central Nepal is hill country, with towns tucked into valleys. And the south is a subtropical[5] river region known as the Terrai.

The country is home to thousands of ancient Hindu and Buddhist temples, eight of the world's 10 tallest mountains, and, some say, the Abominable Snowman.[6] It is also home to 18.7 million citizens, most of whom struggle to extract a living from small plots of land. Ninety-two percent of the Nepalese are farmers. Since almost 80 percent of the country is mountainous, most farming is done by hand, on terraced fields clinging to the sides of steep hills.

Despite its natural beauty, Nepal is one of the world's poorest and most overcrowded countries. Nepalese earn an average of only $160 a year. Life expectancy in Nepal is very low—the average age of death is 52. Diseases that have been wiped out nearly everywhere else on earth, such as leprosy, still plague Nepal.

Competition for Jobs

Many young Nepalese travel to Kathmandu, the country's capital, to look for work. A city of 400,000 surrounded by towering mountains, Kathmandu is the center of what little industry exists in Nepal. But with more than half of Nepal's population under 21, competition for government and manufacturing jobs is intense. Many young people find work

---

4. **strategic:** good for planning and directing efforts
5. **subtropical:** near the earth's hot climate belt
6. **Abominable Snowman:** giant, ape-like beast fabled to live in the Himalayas

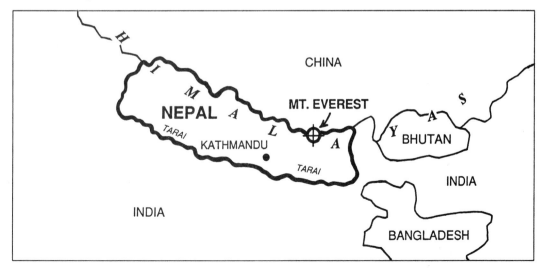

Most farming in Nepal is done on fields cut into steep hillsides.

in Nepal's most profitable industry—tourism.

Each year, over 200,000 tourists travel to Nepal. Drawn by the lure of Mt. Everest, the world's tallest mountain, many come to hike or climb in the Himalayas. Nepalese climbing guides, known as "Sherpas," are considered some of the world's finest mountaineers.

Tourists also come to Nepal to experience its distinctive blend of Asian cultures. The birthplace of Buddhism, Nepal is now 90 percent Hindu. But the Nepalese practice a unique mixture of the two religions. And everywhere one wanders, one encounters Nepalese at worship—often at shrines containing statues of the gods.

Nepalese believe that their leader, King Birendra, is a direct descendant of the gods. Like his father, King Mahendra, who died of a heart attack in 1972, King Birendra dominates Nepalese politics. Nepalese elect representatives to the Panchayat, a parliamentary government based on the British system. But King Birendra has outlawed opposition political parties, and has veto power[7] over all legislation passed by the Panchayat.[8]

One of the Nepalese government's chief challenges is to maintain friendly relations with both India and China. If relations sour with either country, landlocked Nepal is in danger of having its supply of fuel, medicine, and other essential goods cut off. So far, this little kingdom poised on the roof of the world has managed to keep its balance between the two.

---

7. **veto power:** power to reject
8. In response to numerous protests, the government announced the legalization of political parties in 1990. Multi-party elections were scheduled for 1991.

"Exploring the Global Villlage," by David Oliver Relin. From *Scholastic Update*, September 22, 1989.
"Canada: Struggling to Keep Its Identity," by David Strait. From *Scholastic Update*, September 22, 1989.
"Nepal: Poverty amid Soaring Peaks," by David Oliver Relin. From *Scholastic Update*, September 22, 1989.

What do you know about Mexico?
Although rich in cultural traditions and natural resources, Mexico
faces many challenges. Read the following selection to update your
knowledge of one of our nation's closest neighbors.

A. Heine-Stillmark/The Image Bank

Stone carvings on the ruins of a temple in Teotihuacan, Mexico

Mexico

Meeting Challenges

The republic of Mexico, officially the United Mexican States, is a populous, resource-rich nation struggling against forces beyond its control. Plummeting oil prices, devastating earthquakes, and a turbulent history have left their marks on Mexico, but they have not suppressed the Mexican spirit. Mexicans are the inheritors of one of the Western Hemisphere's richest cultural traditions—a blend of Spanish and Indian ways that

may be the source of Mexico's resilient optimism. And Mexico has a lot to be optimistic about: mineral resources of staggering size and variety, a growing industrial capacity, and a modern political stability that seems almost miraculous in light of the nation's stormy past.

The diversity that distinguishes Mexico owes much to the Mexican knack for reaching for the future with one hand while preserving the best from the past with the other. In Mexico's

Aztec ruins uncovered in Mexico City's downtown section during work on the subway system

Mexico City

cities, broad modern plazas lead to ancient Aztec[1] temples, traffic-jammed streets are just minutes away from narrow pack trails, and baseball and bullfights vie for the attention of crowds. Tourists jet in for a sunny vacation beside the awe-inspiring remnants of mighty pre-Columbian[2] Indian civilizations. Elaborate churches rise from the foundations of pagan[3] temples, and broad highways follow the Indian trails along which the conquistadors[4] marched.

Mexico's oil-drilling rigs suggest a recurring Mexican lesson: that a supposed godsend can turn out to be a tragic disappointment. Just as Cortés[5] was not the god some Aztecs are said to have mistaken him for, oil was not the economic savior in the 1970s that it seemed to be. Mexico's rumbling volcanoes suggest yet another lesson: that the geologic forces at work beneath Mexico are extreme. As the disastrous

Mexico City earthquake of 1985 showed, Mexico's greatest challenge may lie in adapting to forces it cannot control while harnessing those it can.

The Land

Mexico is a land of great physical and cultural diversity. With an area of more than 750,000 square miles, it is approximately one-fourth the size of the continental United States (exclusive of Alaska).

Mexico is usually not considered to be part of Central America. On the north is the United States, and the famous Rio Grande of song and story forms part of the border between the two countries. The Gulf of Mexico and the Caribbean

1. **Aztec:** nation of Mexican Indians known for their advanced civilization
2. **pre-Columbian:** from the period before Christopher Columbus's arrival in America in 1492
3. **pagan:** person who worships many gods
4. **conquistadors:** Spaniards who conquered Mexico and other parts of America in the 1500s
5. **Cortés:** Spaniard who conquered the Aztecs

Sea bound Mexico on the east, Guatemala and Belize bound it on the south, and the Pacific Ocean is on the west. The peninsula of Yucatán in eastern Mexico helps divide the Atlantic into the Gulf of Mexico and the Caribbean Sea. Baja California, or Lower California, is a peninsula jutting southward from the state of California.

Mexico is a federal republic[6] divided into 29 states, two territories, and the Federal District of Mexico, which encompasses Mexico City. When Mexicans speak of "Mexico," they mean Mexico City; they refer to the country as a whole as "the republic."

Physical Features

Much of Mexico is mountainous. Two great mountain chains, the Sierra Madre Occidental and the Sierra Madre Oriental, extend along Mexico's west and east coasts, respectively. A number of valleys and plateaus of differing altitudes lie among these mountains. The Central Plateau, Mexico's topographical[7] heartland, is located between these two ranges. This plateau comprises more than half of Mexico's land area. From north to south, the Central Plateau gradually rises in altitude from about 3,600 feet near the U.S. border to about 8,000 feet in some of the southern intermountain basins. Most of the principal cities are located on this plateau, and here the density of population is greatest, especially in the sections near Mexico City. It is also the chief agricultural region.

Climate

North Americans think of Mexico as very hot, but this is not true throughout the country. Because of the varying altitudes and because the country lies partly in the temperate zone[8] and partly in the tropical zone,[9] its climate ranges from tropical to cool. There are two seasons: it is rainy from June to October and dry from November to May. The rainfall, like the temperature, varies considerably with the altitude. The low country along the coasts, on the Yucatán Peninsula, and on the Isthmus of Tehuantepec is humid, while semi-arid highland plains cover much of the north. The average temperature of the plateau region is from 60 degrees to 70 degrees Fahrenheit, and on the coastal plains it ranges from 80 degrees to 90 degrees Fahrenheit.

The People

Mexico's population is large and growing. In 1985, the population of Mexico was estimated at 80 million. According to some estimates, by the year 2100 Mexico could have as many as 195 million people and could be the tenth most populous country in the world. The central area of the country, especially in and around Mexico City, is the most densely populated. The population of the Federal District, which includes Mexico City, nearly doubled between 1974 and 1986 and stands now at more than 15 million people, making it one of the largest urban areas in the Western Hemisphere. The movement of people away from traditionally agricultural areas

---

6. **federal republic:** union of states with a central government where power is given to representatives elected by the people
7. **topographical:** having to do with the physical features of the land
8. **temperate zone:** mild climate belt between the tropical and polar regions
9. **tropical zone:** very hot climate belt near the equator

Women work in a shoe factory in Leon, a city in central Mexico, where the shoe industry is a main source of income.

are also a source of great wealth, for most of the country's metal ores lie buried in the mountains. The chief metallic minerals are silver, lead, and zinc, but gold, copper, sulfur, cadmium, and other minerals are plentiful. Most of Mexico's mineral production is for export, partly because the country's domestic economy is not yet sufficiently developed to consume it. The exceptions are coal and iron, which are used by Mexican factories.

Petroleum is one of Mexico's most valuable resources. Foreign investors, mainly British and American, were the first to develop and industrialize Mexico's petroleum reserves on a large scale. What seemed at the time to be extraordinarily large reserves were discovered, and Mexico became, in the early twentieth century, the world's

to the large cities reflects the number of former agricultural workers now involved in industry and trade. Only about one-third of the Mexican people still live in rural areas.

Mining

Since the Spanish conquest, minerals have traditionally been Mexico's greatest source of wealth. Up until the last few decades, however, the exploitation of Mexico's minerals brought little benefit to the Mexicans themselves. The Spaniards virtually enslaved the Indian population, put them to work in the mines, and robbed Mexico of its mineral riches, especially silver.

Although Mexico's mountains are economic obstacles in many ways, they

A plant in Minatitlan, Mexico, that processes petroleum

Mexico's beaches are popular with tourists. On this beach sits a sculpture created by the Toltecs, an Indian civilization that existed in Mexico more than 1000 years ago.

second largest producer of petroleum. Since the late 1920s, petroleum production has increased, but Mexico's proportionate share of the world market has declined because of the development of fields in other regions, notably the Middle East.

In 1939 the Mexican government nationalized[10] the oil industry so that enormous profits would not continue to be taken out of the country. In the years since, Mexico has directed the development of its own oil reserves through a state-subsidized company, Petróleos Mexicanos (Pemex).

Tourism

Tourism is a major source of national income. Cancún on the Gulf of Mexico and Mazatlán, Puerto Vallarta, and Acapulco on the Pacific attract thousands of tourists from all over the world, principally from the United States. Many U.S. tourists also visit Mexican cities like Tijuana, Matamoros, and Nogales, which lie just across the border from cities in the United States. Inland places such as Guadalajara (with nearby Lake Chapala), Cuernavaca, and Mérida, are also popular.

---

10. **nationalized:** put under control of the national government

---

From *Mexico in Pictures,* Geography Department, Lerner Communications.

Is the earth's environment as fragile as news reports suggest? The following selection presents a point of view that may suprise you. As you read, consider how the survival of humankind depends on protecting the environment.

CLEANING UP OUR MESS

A swirl of oil in Alaska's Prince William Sound two weeks after the Exxon *Valdez* oil spill

In the aftermath of events like the Exxon *Valdez*[1] oil spill, every reference to the environment is prefaced with the adjective "fragile." Nothing could be further from the truth.

The environment is nearly indestructible. It has survived ice ages, bombardments of cosmic radiation, fluctuations of the sun, reversals of the seasons caused by shifts in the planetary axis, collisions of comets and meteors bearing far more force than our doomsday arsenals, and

---

1. **Exxon *Valdez*:** tanker ship that ran aground in Prince William Sound along the coast of Alaska in March 1989

lightless "nuclear winters" that followed these impacts. Though mischievous, human assaults are pinpricks compared with forces of the magnitude nature is accustomed to resisting.

One aspect of the environment is genuinely delicate, though. Namely, the set of conditions favorable to human beings. Earth's ecosphere[2] is ever in flux.[3] Climates, configurations of the continents, dominant biological and chemical forces shift endlessly. A scant 20,000 years ago the rivers and lakes we now fret about preserving did not exist: retreating glaciers had yet to carve them. Turn back a few pages and none of the rain forests or wilderness tracts we fear "irrevocably" losing existed to lose; nor did the vast majority of current plants and animals; nor did any human forebear.[4]

To Mother Nature our contemporary infatuation with endangered species must seem callow sentimentality, for extinction is the environment's norm: 99 percent of the creatures ever to have come into existence have vanished. Nature doesn't care if the globe is populated by trilobites or thunder lizards or people or six-eyed telepathic slugs. What nature cares about is that the ecosystem[5] *live*. Should we sour the environmental conditions now slanted in our favor, creatures will rise up in our stead that thrive on murky greenhouse air, or dine on compounds human metabolisms find toxic. The full measure of the ecosystem's toughness is how little it needs us, the sea otters of Prince William Sound, or any particular creature.

In the modern world, even if a nation renders its own environment clean, no amount of wealth or military strength may enable it to escape the side effects of environmental abuses elsewhere. Inevitably, this suggests the coming century will hold either general environmental misfortune, the distress to be suffered everywhere, or increased environmental cooperation, the benefits to be shared by rich and poor alike. Perhaps the environment, the place where we all must live, will become the bond that finally brings the nations of the world together.

Though the subject is complex, readers should be of cheer: the environment *can* be understood, and the path for improvements can be lighted.

---

2. **ecosphere:** zone in which life can exist
3. **flux:** continuous change or movement
4. **forebear:** ancestor
5. **ecosystem:** all living and nonliving things in an area and the relationships among them

---

"Cleaning up Our Mess," by Gregg Easterbrook. From *Newsweek,* July 12, 1989.

Do you ever long to travel for a change of season? Read to discover one person's dream of escaping winter and traveling with the spring through the eastern United States.

Harald Sund/The Image Bank

North with the Spring

Bare trees imprinted the black lace of their twigs on a gray and somber sky. Dingy with soot, snowdrifts had melted into slush and were freezing again. Behind us, as we drove south, city pallor[1] was increasing. Tempers were growing short in the dead air of underventilated offices. That quiet desperation, which Thoreau[2] says characterizes the mass of men, was taking on new intensity. February, at once the shortest and the longest month of the 12, had outstayed its welcome. The year seemed stuck on the ridge of winter.

---

1. **pallor:** paleness
2. **Thoreau:** American writer known for works on social protest and living in harmony with nature

At such a time, when you look with dread upon the winter weeks that lie before you, have you ever dreamed—in office or kitchen or school—of leaving winter behind, of meeting spring under far-southern skies, of following its triumphal pilgrimage[3] up the map with flowers all the way, with singing birds and soft air, green grass and trees new-clothed, of coming north with the spring? That is a dream of the winter-weary. And, for nearly a decade, it was, for Nellie and me, both a dream and a plan.

The seasons, like greater tides, ebb and flow across the continents. Spring advances up the United States at the average rate of about 15 miles a day. It ascends mountainsides at the rate of about 100 feet a day. It sweeps ahead like a flood of water, racing down the long valleys, creeping up hillsides in a rising tide. Most of us, like the man who lives on the bank of a river and watches the stream flow by, see only one phase of the movement of spring. Each year the season advances toward us out of the south, sweeps around us, goes flooding away into the north. We see all phases of a single phase, all variations of this one chapter in the Odyssey[4] of Spring. My wife and I dreamed of knowing something of all phases, of reading all possible chapters, of seeing, firsthand, the long northward flow of the season.

Over and over again we laid out routes, calculated costs, made lists of things to take along. But obligations and responsibilities pushed the dream unrealized before us. Season followed season and year followed year. And while we waited, the world changed and our lives changed with it. The spring trip was something we looked forward to during the terrible years of World War II, during all the strain and grief of losing David, our only son, in battle.

When we talked over our plans with friends we discovered that our dream was a universal[5] dream. They, too, had beguiled[6] themselves, on days when winter seemed invincible, with thoughts of lifting anchor and, leaving everyday responsibilities behind, drifting north with the spring.

Our plan was to start where spring begins for the North American continent, somewhere south of Lake Okeechobee in that no-man's-land of the seasons, the Everglades. There, amid the sawgrass seas and hammocks, under the high, cloud-filled sky of southern Florida, spring

---

3. pilgrimage: journey to a sacred place
4. Odyssey: adventurous travels
5. universal: existing everywhere
6. beguiled: passed time pleasantly

gathers its forces. There, the first stirrings of the season become apparent. Working north, we would keep pace with its progress, zigzagging by car behind its advancing front. Above the peninsula of Florida we would swing wide along the Gulf to the Louisiana marshes, cut back to the Okefenokee Swamp, then trail the season through the Great Smokies, across the Piedmont Plateau, among the Jersey pine barrens, out to the tip of Cape Cod and through the mountains of New England to the green boundary of the Canadian line. I ruled off a map into zones, each zone representing roughly a week's advance in the northward movement of the season. This provided, in general, the timetable of our trip.

Ours would be no conventional tour. It would include wild and remote places the usual tourist avoids. We would see spring come to dunes and tarns and seashell islands, to caves and underground rivers, to estuaries and savannas. For 17,000 miles we would travel with a season. In 23 different states we would witness the defeat of winter, see the homecoming of the birds, watch the return of the wildflowers. This was the long spring. It would extend from February to June. The trip, for me, would have added pleasure because my companion, after years of married life, was the most congenial person still.

And so, on the 14th of February, we packed our black Buick, stuffed the glove compartment full of marked maps, stored away bird glasses, field guides, cameras, and stoutly-bound record books. We eased ourselves into the front seat like a racing pilot squeezing into the cramped cockpit of a speedplane and waved goodbye to our neighbors. I switched on the engine, and we started south for our rendezvous[7] with a season.

Long Island was hard with frost when we left. New York was a world of windows tight shut. Across New Jersey, the distant winter woods were smoky blue and, in Virginia, side roads cut away between brown hills, rutted and red. We saw the white sand of South Carolina pinelands replaced by the copper-colored soil of Georgia. We watched mistletoe give way to Spanish moss and Spanish moss give way to air plants in the cypress swamps of southern Florida. Our descent of the map ended south of the Tamiami Trail, at the little community of Everglades, near the Ten Thousand Islands of the wild Gulf coast. Here we reached the beginning of our travels with the spring.

---

7. rendezvous: meeting or appointment to meet

From *North with the Spring*, by Edwin Way Teale.

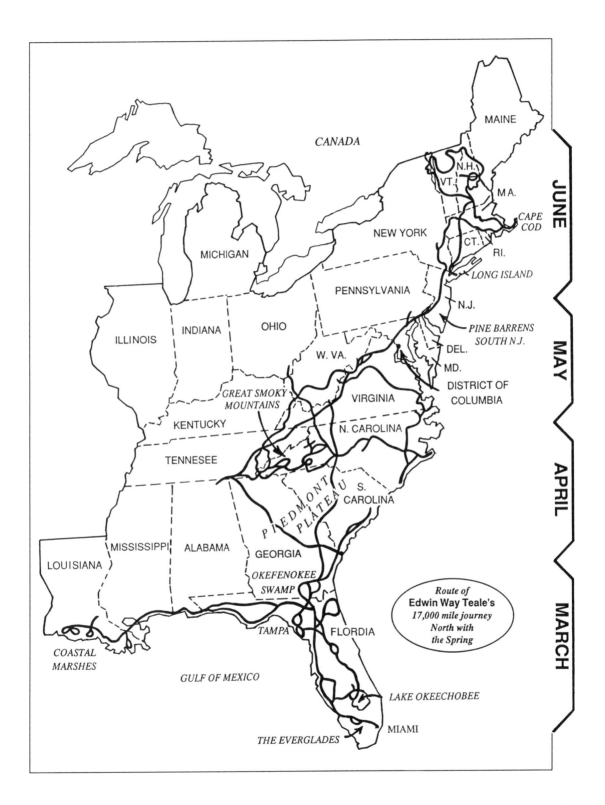

The Everglades · Miami · Lake Okeechobee · Tampa · Florida · Gulf of Mexico · Coastal Marshes · Louisiana · Mississippi · Alabama · Georgia · Okefenokee Swamp · Piedmont Plateau · S. Carolina · Tennessee · Kentucky · Illinois · Indiana · Ohio · W. Va. · Great Smoky Mountains · Virginia · N. Carolina · Michigan · New York · Pennsylvania · Canada · Maine · N.H. · VT · MA. · Cape Cod · CT. · RI. · Long Island · N.J. · Pine Barrens South N.J. · Del. · Md. · District of Columbia

JUNE · MAY · APRIL · MARCH

Route of
Edwin Way Teale's
*17,000 mile journey
North with
the Spring*

Andy Caulfield/The Image Bank

This Land Is Your Land

This land is your land, this land is my land,
From California to the New York island,
From the redwood forest to the Gulf Stream waters,
This land was made for you and me.

As I was walking that ribbon of highway,
I saw above me that endless skyway,
I saw below me that golden valley.
This land was made for you and me.

I've roamed and rambled and I followed my footsteps
To the sparkling sands of her diamond deserts,
And all around me a voice was sounding,
"This land was made for you and me."

When the sun came shining and I was strolling,
And the wheat fields waving and the dust clouds rolling,
As the fog was lifting, a voice was chanting,
"This land was made for you and me."

Unit 2: History

the study of past events

MY FATHER REMINISCES, 1937, Ida Abelman
National Museum of American Art, Washington, DC/Art Resource, NY

Do too many Americans take free public education for granted?
When the United States began, many people had no chance at all to
attend school. As you read the following selection, think about how
educational opportunities have grown through the years.

COUNTRY SCHOOL, E.L. Henry, Yale University Art Gallery,
The Mabel Brady Garvan Collection, Photograph by Joseph Szaszfai'

The Development of U.S. Education

The Colonial Period

Most colonists who came to America set up the kinds of schools they had known in Europe. Protestants and Roman Catholics established and supported their own schools. Most were elementary schools designed to teach reading, writing, and religion. School attendance was not compulsory in the colonies. Only about one child out of 10 went to school. Many children learned a trade by becoming apprentices.[1] The children of wealthier colonists studied under tutors or were sent to tuition schools[2] or to schools in England.

In 1642, the Massachusetts Bay Colony, the largest New England colony, passed a law requiring parents to teach their children to read. In 1647, Massachusetts passed the first law in America requiring communities to establish public schools. The law

---

1. **apprentices:** people who learn a trade by working with a skilled worker
2. **tuition schools:** schools requiring payment to attend

required every town with at least 50 families to start an elementary school, and every town of 100 families or more to have a Latin grammar school. Like other colonial schools, these town schools taught religion. But unlike other schools in the colonies, they were partially supported by public funds. The elementary schools were open to all children. The grammar schools were attended mainly by boys preparing for college. The Boston Latin School, which opened in 1635, was the first Latin grammar school—and the first secondary school of any kind—in the colonies.

Secondary schools called *academies* were started in many of the colonies during the 1700s. Academies offered more practical courses than did Latin grammar schools. A student could take such subjects as bookkeeping and navigation in addition to religion and liberal arts[3] courses. Most academies were private schools supported by tuition fees. Some admitted girls, and some were established for girls only.

In 1636, Massachusetts founded Harvard College, the first institution of higher learning in the colonies. By the early 1800s, the school had become Harvard University. When the Revolutionary War ended in 1783, the United States had 18 institutions of higher learning. Several were partially state supported and controlled. In 1785, Georgia chartered[4] the first state university, but it did not open until 1801.

---

3. liberal arts: subjects that give a general education rather than a scientific or technical one
4. chartered: gave official support for

A school in Wisconsin around the years 1890–1910
Van Schaick Collection. Photo by Charles Van Schaick. State Historical Society of Wisconsin

Saluting the American flag in a school in New York around the years 1889–1890
Photograph by Jacob A. Riis. Jacob A. Riis Collection, Museum of the City of New York

In 1795, North Carolina University became the first state university to hold classes.

The 1800s

After the Revolutionary War, many Americans were concerned with unifying the nation. Attempts to promote unity had two important effects on education: (1) the development of standardized[5] textbooks and (2) the building of state public school systems.

During the 1700s and early 1800s, a number of educators produced books designed specifically for Americans. Noah Webster's famous "Blue-Backed Speller" helped standardize spelling and pronunciation in the United States. Millions of elementary school students used illustrated reading books published by William H. McGuffey. These "McGuffey Readers" taught patriotism and helped form literary tastes in the United States.

Patriotism was only one element the early American educators stressed. They also emphasized that good Americans were deeply religious—and were preferably Protestants. Good Americans were also honest, thrifty, hardworking, and courageous. In trying to develop an idealized view of Americans, the early educators often tended to describe other people as lacking in these traits. This tendency was reflected in the textbooks developed for school use. Most American authors saw the English, Scottish, German, and Swiss people as somewhat like themselves and thus highly admirable. But people whose way of life

---

5. **standardized:** made to meet a regular standard

differed considerably from their own were described unfavorably. Authors often described Spaniards, for example, as unusually cruel and lazy. They said the American Indians—though noble and loyal to their own group—were savages who could not be civilized. Yet many peoples throughout history have used their schools in this way to give children a sense of their nation's greatness.

The textbooks and other teaching materials were thus designed to unify the American people. But in the early 1800s, an increasing number of people came to believe that something more was needed to give Americans common goals and a sense of national unity. They felt the answer lay in public education and proposed that each state set up a system of free, compulsory, tax-supported schools. They wanted the schools to be free of religious control but devoted to building character and teaching patriotism.

However, certain religious groups, especially Roman Catholics and Lutherans, disliked some of the principles taught in the public schools. As a result, they maintained and controlled alternate schools. Some people, particularly the very wealthy, disliked the fact that the public schools tended to equalize everyone. They continued to send their children to private schools. But for generations, immigrants from many countries and of many religions found the public schools a path into the mainstream of American life.

In 1837, Massachusetts established a state board of education to coordinate its public school system. The Massachusetts board became a model for similar boards in many other states. The first secretary of the Massachusetts board, the educator Horace Mann, did much to strengthen education in the state. Under his leadership, Massachusetts began the nation's first public normal school[6] in 1839. In 1852, the Massachusetts legislature passed the first compulsory school-attendance law in the United States. By the end of the 1800s, 31 of the 45 states had school-attendance laws. By 1918, every state had such a law.

Boston opened the nation's first public high school in 1821. But some people believed that the use of public funds to support secondary schools was illegal. This question was largely settled by a Michigan Supreme Court decision in 1874. The court ruled that local governments could use tax money to support secondary schools as well as elementary schools.

Higher education also made many advances during the 1800s. Churches and other private organizations founded several hundred small liberal arts colleges in the 1800s. In an 1819 decision, the U.S. Supreme Court had prohibited the states from taking over private colleges. In 1862, Congress passed the Morrill, or Land-Grant, Act, which gave vast areas of federal land to the states. The act required each state to sell the land and use the proceeds to start agricultural and technical colleges. In 1833, Oberlin Collegiate Institute (now Oberlin College) in Ohio became the first coeducational[7] college in the United States.

---

6. **normal school:** school for training high-school graduates to become teachers
7. **coeducational:** for both male and female students

The Early 1900s

The early 1900s brought far-reaching changes in U.S. education. A number of educators in the 1800s paved the way for these reforms. Margaretha Schurz, the wife of political leader Carl Schurz, opened the nation's first private kindergarten in 1856 in Watertown, Wisconsin. William T. Harris helped establish the nation's first public kindergarten in St. Louis in 1873. Kindergartens used play and creative activities as teaching methods. Francis W. Parker, an Illinois educator, adopted these methods for use in elementary schools. The teaching methods used in many schools in the 1800s stressed memorization and discipline. Parker believed education's chief goal should be the complete development of every child, and more freedom was needed to achieve this goal. Parker and other educators broadened elementary school courses by adding such subjects as geography, history, and science.

The new child-centered theories of education influenced many educators who felt that the schools had not kept up with changes in society. These educators proposed that teachers adopt such methods as field trips, group discussions, and creative activities to help prepare children for life in a democracy. John Dewey and William H. Kilpatrick were two of the principal supporters of such ideas, which became known as *progressive education.*

Joliet Junior College, the nation's oldest junior college, opened in Joliet, Illinois, in 1901. About 1910, several U.S. cities built the first junior high schools. Vocational[8] education developed rapidly after Congress passed the Smith-Hughes Act in 1917. The act granted the states federal funds for vocational education in the fields of agriculture, home economics, and industrial arts.

The Great Depression and World War II

A decline in the U.S. birth rate during the 1920s contributed to a decrease in elementary school enrollments during the economic depression of the 1930s. But high school and college enrollments climbed as many young people unable to get jobs continued their education.

School enrollments dropped at all levels after the United States entered World War II in 1941. Many high school and college students enlisted in the armed forces or were drafted. Many others went to work in war industries. A greatly increased birth rate in the years immediately following World War II led to a rapid rise in elementary school enrollments in the 1950s.

The Mid-1900s

The U.S. educational system experienced a number of changes during the mid-1900s. Larger school enrollments after World War II created a need for more school buildings, and inflation increased the cost of constructing and operating schools. Teachers' organizations became more militant[9] as they bargained for improved benefits for their members. Teacher militancy led to a record number of strikes in the late 1960s and early 1970s. Partly as a result

---

8. **vocational:** related to an occupation or trade
9. **militant:** aggressive

An American classroom of recent years

of these efforts, the average annual salary of U.S. schoolteachers increased by more than 70 percent between 1960 and 1970.

The federal government greatly increased its financial aid to education during the mid-1900s. After World War II, for example, Congress began granting federal funds to armed forces veterans to attend colleges and other schools. This program helped more than 10 million veterans continue their education after leaving service.

The Elementary and Secondary Education Act, passed by Congress in 1965, furnished local school districts with funds to help educate children from low-income families. In 1981, the act became known as the Educational Consolidation and Improvement Act. Large sums of money for higher education were provided by the National Defense Education Act of 1958, the Higher Education Facilities Act of 1963, the Higher Education Act of 1965, and the Education Amendments Act of 1972.

Recent Developments

Enrollment in U.S. elementary and secondary schools began to decline during the 1970s. Declining enrollment forced many schools to close during the early 1980s. In addition, many other schools suffered financially because of reduced federal aid to education. These cuts in funding were due to the government's efforts to balance the federal budget.

Other important developments in U.S. education include efforts to guarantee equal educational opportunities to minority groups and to provide public funds to parochial[10] schools.

---

10. parochial: associated with a church

Excerpted from *The World Book Encyclopedia.*
© 1990 World Book, Inc. By permission of the publisher.

How can strong leadership help during a crisis? When Franklin Delano Roosevelt ran for president in 1932, the nation was in the midst of the severe economic crisis known as the Great Depression. Roosevelt promised the American people a "New Deal" if he were elected. Read to discover how President Roosevelt set his New Deal plans into action.

Franklin Roosevelt giving a radio fireside chat

The First New Deal

FDR awoke his first morning in the White House unaccustomed to the blank walls of the bedroom and the set of newspapers that lay at his bedside. After breakfast, he went to the Oval Room where his presidential office would be and gazed at the blank surface of his desk. He could find no pencil or paper in the empty drawers, not even a buzzer to ring for a secretary.

Not a soul seemed to be around to assist him, and this was no way to get things done. Suddenly the president leaned back in his chair, opened his mouth wide, and let out a huge yell. Secretaries, aides, staff, all came running. The president had called for action, and the momentum of the First Hundred Days was about to begin.

He had already chosen his Cabinet officers,[1] and they had turned their attention first to the banking crisis. Two measures were already prepared to deal with the crisis, since many banks throughout the country had already collapsed financially. The first measure the

---

1. Cabinet officers: government department heads who are the president's official advisers

president took was the drastic step of declaring a bank holiday, closing the doors of every bank in the nation. His plan was to reopen them gradually on a sounder basis.

This shocked and bewildered the people whose savings were already dwindling and now were locked away completely. The president knew he had to explain this action to the people to restore their confidence in the banking community, so he went before the public in his first radio fireside chat. In warm and simple terms he explained just how he would deal with the banks. He then called Congress into special session and proposed his Emergency Banking Act to open banks under an orderly and licensed system.

His talk on the radio and his direct action with Congress generated a fresh mood of hope among the people. Some called it a wave of sunlight, for now citizens knew that bold action would be used to renew the country.

FDR sensed the mood of the people and Congress. He had them on his side, and now was the time to move ahead to enact the new laws that were needed. So in the next hundred days he pushed through a torrent of important bills to set forces moving toward recovery.

With public opinion solidly behind him, he warned Congress that the national crisis called for emergency measures, and the bills poured forth. First came an Economy Bill to cut government costs and balance the federal budget as he had promised to do if elected. Then other proposals and plans followed in rapid order. In 100 days he made 10 speeches, sent Congress 15 messages, pushed through many laws, talked to reporters at twice-weekly press conferences, and conferred constantly with influential men. Through all the hard work he displayed a remarkable brand of confidence and good cheer that amazed all who worked with him.

These were the bills that he handed to Congress those First Hundred Days:

March 9	Emergency Banking Act	May 18	Tennessee Valley Authority Act
March 20	Economy Act	May 27	Truth-in-Securities Act
March 31	Civilian Conservation Corps	June 13	Home Owner's Loan Act
April 19	Gold Standard abandoned (ratified June 5)	June 16	National Industrial Recovery Act Glass-Steagall Banking Act Farm Credit Act
May 12	Federal Emergency Relief Act Emergency Farm Mortgage Act		

Just after the president's inauguration, Will Rogers[2] had said, "America hasn't been as happy in three years as they are today. No money, no banks, no work, no nothing, but they know they got a man in there who is wise to Congress, wise to our so-called big men. The whole country is with him." The people felt that FDR's New Deal was trying to deal a new deck of cards that would not be stacked against them.

FDR liked and knew how to work with people. At the beginning of his term, a ragged army of poor and hungry veterans of World War I marched on Washington to demand money for their Army service. They had done the same when Hoover was president, and Hoover had called out the Army to disband their camp and burn down their tents. When they marched on Roosevelt, he promptly sent doctors, food, coffee, tents, the Navy band to play for them, and his wife to talk with them. Eleanor marched through the mud of their camp and sang songs with them.

"Hoover sent the Army; Roosevelt sent his wife," they all said, and most of them joined the Civilian Conservation Corps or went home. This was the emotion he inspired.

His Civilian Conservation Corps pulled young men off the streets and gave them jobs that would help build up the country. By June of that year, camps all over the country housed young men who worked to plant forests, construct dams, or build parks. The health and morale of these boys improved quickly, although they had not eaten well or lived

Forestry workers in the Civilian Conservation Corps clear ground for a campsite near Luray, Virginia.

2. **Will Rogers:** American humorist and social critic

decently for some time. Part of their wages were sent home to families, and by the coming of winter, fewer people had the same dread of cold and hunger that many had felt the year before.

The Federal Emergency Relief Act provided 500 million dollars to improve roads, build schools, airports, parks, and sewer systems. FDR saw to it that money found its way directly to the people so they could buy food and clothes and earn self-respect by working again. Money was spent on reforestation, flood control, water works, sewage plants,

Unemployed people line up outside the State Labor Building in New York City to try to get Federal Relief jobs.

and slum clearance. Artists, musicians, writers, and white-collar workers were hired to write histories of their communities, paint murals for post offices, and catalog libraries. A federal theater project employed actors and writers to write and produce plays. Gradually, people gained new hope and purpose as Roosevelt's New Deal took hold.

The president created an even grander scheme to join business and government for the common good. New Dealers felt that if every factory, shop, and business voluntarily agreed to draw up codes of fair practice, regulate wages and work hours, forbid child labor, and agree to enforce such codes, the economy would benefit. So the National Industrial Recovery Act was born, and soon its symbol, a blue eagle clutching a cogwheel, and the slogan "We Do Our Part," was plastered on store windows and on the products of some 700 industries that joined the National Recovery Administration (NRA). The President had great hopes for his plan.

Later the NRA would be declared unconstitutional, but before it was outlawed it made progress in improving living and working conditions.

It got rid of many sweatshops,[3] removed many young children from miserable toil in factories, helped organized labor get a bigger share of what it produced, and induced people to think more in terms of national planning and cooperation between business and labor.

The plight of the farmer was almost worse than that of the factory worker. Farmers were earning so little money they could not afford even the rock-bottom prices of consumer products. Bread cost five cents a loaf, tomatoes eight pounds for five cents, lettuce a penny a pound, sliced bacon 10 cents a pound, and sirloin steak 20 cents a pound, but hardly any farmer was able to afford even these prices.

Sharecroppers[4] of the South who rented a bit of land from a large landowner lived in misery. And the disaster of drought in the early 1930s brought a dust bowl to the prairie states, with soil parched and cracked until the wind blew choking black clouds across the dry earth. The helpless farmer watched his crops wither away and his cattle die for lack of water.

The farmers had made so little money on their crops that they could not make payments on their farms. But men who had worked land for years refused to give up their property and stood in their barnyards, shotgun in hand, to ward off any forecloser[5] who came to demand

The Bettmann Archive

A farmhouse in the vicinity of Dalhart, Texas, stands abandoned during the Dust Bowl of the 1930s.

---

3. sweatshops: places where people work under poor conditions for low pay
4. sharecroppers: farmers who work for a share of the crop
5. forecloser: lender who can take over a property if money borrowed to buy that property is not paid as agreed

payment. The president knew that violence could break out at any time, and he halted the foreclosing of mortgages and gave the farmers loans to preserve their farms.

Perhaps one of the greatest achievements of the First Hundred Days was the law passed to create the Tennessee Valley Authority. This law brought to reality a dream of abundance and well-being for several million people who had been living in poverty. The plan was to control a mighty river through a system of dams.

Ultimately, the TVA brought cheap and plentiful electricity, inland waterways for better transportation, and nitrate plants that produced inexpensive fertilizer for farmers.

Altogether, the First Hundred Days of Roosevelt's Administration were as exciting and productive as any in the history of the nation. The measures passed during that period started a chain of legislation and action that significantly changed the course of American life in the twentieth century. For the first two years of his term Roosevelt rode a great wave of popularity. And when Congressional election time came in 1934, the people responded by giving Roosevelt's Democrats an even greater majority in both Houses of Congress.

But as with all popular administrations, the honeymoon did not last forever. After 1934 there were increasing signs of resistance to the president. Business began to turn away from him, and FDR looked instead to farmers, laborers, and poor people as a base of support.

Of course, the measures passed during the first years of the New Deal did not immediately solve all the problems of the Depression. Consumer buying power did not rise fast enough. Businessmen did not fully cooperate on regulating prices. Employers continued to cut wages as they saw fit.

He always kept an ear attuned to public opinion. He listened carefully to Eleanor when she reported the situation of the people after one of her frequent fact-finding trips. "Look at the condition of their clothes on the wash line...notice their cars," he told her, and he would always ask what people were eating, how they lived, and what their farms looked like.

By 1935 increased pressures from the left[6] forced him to join more closely with the progressive[7] elements of the party and with a Congress

---

6. **the left:** groups whose political views favor the rights of the individual and using government power to promote social progress
7. **progressive:** favoring active political and social reform

that passed the Wagner Bill to give greater power to labor. One of the most important bills of the New Deal went through Congress in 1935. This was the Social Security Act to give greater aid to the aged and help the unemployed, blind, and crippled, and dependent mothers and children.

The Social Security system continues today.

But as FDR and Congress moved toward the left, the nine men who sat as judges on the United States Supreme Court were moving in the opposite direction. In 1935 they considered a host of cases to decide if it was constitutional for the federal government to wield the great power FDR had used in passing New Deal laws. The court decided that some of this federal power was unconstitutional and that Congress could not give the president such authority. Although many New Deal measures were held to be legal, the Supreme Court ruled that some were not. The court not only declared the NRA unconstitutional, but it also found the Agricultural Adjustment Act[8] an invasion of states' rights.

---

8. Agricultural Adjustment Act: legislation passed in May 1933 that limited crop production in order to raise prices of agricultural products. Farmers were paid to lower production and penalized if they produced too much.

From *Franklin Delano Roosevelt: President of the People,* by Roslyn and Ray Hiebert.

Are rights given freely, or must people fight for them?
This selection outlines the struggle for civil rights by African-Americans.
As you read consider the methods used to bring about change.

Outside a railroad station in Jackson, Mississippi, 1955

AP/Wide World Photos

CIVIL RIGHTS

Civil rights can be defined as those basic freedoms and privileges—the right to vote, to hold and express opinions freely, to receive due process[1] of law in criminal cases, etc.—that a government grants its citizens. Having lived under the tyranny of a monarchy,[2] the framers of the Constitution understood that government must protect its citizens' civil rights if democracy is to flourish. The Bill of Rights still stands as probably the most direct expression of civil rights in history.

But civil rights for whom? When the Constitution was ratified,[3] women had no legal rights, almost all blacks were slaves, and few people besides white, landowning males participated in government. In many ways the history of civil rights in America has been a struggle to ensure that the rights expressed in the Constitution apply to all Americans—regardless of race, sex, or creed.

---

1. **due process:** proper legal course
2. **monarchy:** government ruled by a king, queen, or emperor
3. **ratified:** approved

The best-known struggle for civil rights has been that of the nation's largest minority, black Americans. During Reconstruction,[4] blacks—freed by the Thirteenth Amendment, and, at least in theory, citizens—were often repressed as badly as they had been under slavery. Bitter, defeated white southerners sought to deprive blacks of their civil rights through terror and intimidation. Lynching[5] was common and organizations such as the Ku Klux Klan flourished. The need for protection of black rights, particularly the right to vote, led to the creation of the Freedmen's Bureau and the passage of the Fourteenth and Fifteenth Amendments[6] and the Civil Rights Acts of 1866 and 1871. None of these was particularly successful. In 1888, the Supreme Court case of *Plessy* v. *Ferguson* ruled that segregation[7] by race in public accommodations was constitutional as long as the facilities were "separate but equal." They rarely were.

The next half-century saw little progress in civil rights for blacks. Despite the formation of the NAACP (the National Association for the Advancement of Colored People), an organization dedicated to black rights, and a favorable ruling on black voting in the Supreme Court case of *Nixon* v. *Herndon,* black Americans remained largely disenfranchised;[8] they were still lacking in opportunity, and prevented from participating in government at even the most basic level.

In the early 1950s, the struggle for civil rights was fought primarily in the federal courts. Soon events began that would result in a widespread and vocal movement for civil rights. In 1954, in *Brown* v. *Board of Education,* the Supreme Court ruled against school segregation. In an important test of this ruling, President Eisenhower ordered federal troops to enforce the Court's decision when Little Rock, Arkansas, refused to admit black students to its schools. In 1955, in Montgomery, Alabama, black citizens, led by a young minister, Dr. Martin Luther King, Jr., conducted a successful boycott[9] of a bus company to protest discrimination in public transportation.

The civil rights movement grew in strength and size in the next decade. Demonstrations, from sit-ins at segregated lunch counters to the massive marches on Washington, D.C. and Selma, Alabama, led by Martin Luther King, Jr., focused the nation's attention on the struggle for equality. Congress passed a number of laws—including the Civil Rights Act of 1964, the Voting Rights Act, and the Poll Tax Amendment—to end discrimination against blacks and protect their right to participate in government. King was felled by an assassin in 1968, but the struggle continued.

---

4. **Reconstruction:** period (1865–1877) when the Union restored relations with the defeated Southern states after the Civil War
5. **lynching:** putting a person to death without a lawful trial
6. **Fourteenth and Fifteenth Amendments:** The Fourteenth Amendment, passed in 1868, declared all people born or naturalized in the United States to be citizens with equal protection of the laws. The Fifteenth Amendment, passed in 1870, declared that the right to vote could not be denied because of race.
7. **segregation:** separating one group from another
8. **disenfranchised:** deprived of rights, especially the right to vote
9. **boycott:** agreement not to do business with someone in order to punish or to force a change

Dr. Martin Luther King, Jr., (hand pointing) in the Selma-to-Montgomery civil rights march in Alabama, 1965

In the 1970s, the struggle moved back to the federal courts and the Supreme Court upheld the practice of busing children to schools outside their neighborhoods to achieve integration.[10] The late 1970s and the 1980s also saw criticism of legal safeguards for civil rights; some people felt measures such as affirmative action[11] and quotas for minority employment and education fostered "discrimination in reverse"—an issue the Supreme Court addressed in the Bakke case.[12]

The movement for civil rights has made great strides in the last quarter-century, but much remains to be done if true equality for all Americans—regardless of their race, religion, and beliefs—is to be achieved. Civil rights legislation does not always mean a better life for minorities, and legal equality does not automatically assure increased opportunity; members of minority groups still have a far higher rate of poverty and unemployment than the white majority.

10. **integration:** bringing together people of different races or ethnic groups
11. **affirmative action:** policies for correcting effects of discrimination in employment or education
12. **Bakke case:** 1978 case that the Supreme Court decided in favor of a white man named Allan Bakke. The University of California Medical School at Davis had refused to admit Bakke. He later learned his grades and test scores were higher than those of several people admitted under a special program for minorities, and he sued the university on grounds of racial discrimination.

From *Key Issues in Constitutional History*, edited by C. Carter Smith.

Mai Vang (right) and her children Pang (center) and Noel (left) hoe their vegetable field.

Photo by Walter Kale

BACK to the LAND

Is it hard to begin a life in a new place? The following selection concerns a group of refugees from Laos who settled in the United States after the Vietnam War. As you read about one family's experiences, consider their ability to survive and to adjust to life in a new land.

In the cool of the morning, as the roosters crow and the golden sun begins its ascent in the sky, Mai Vang, in a straw hat and beat-up winter boots, is already at work on her farm on the high plains of Minnesota. With a short-handled triangular hoe, she bends over rows of sugar snap peas, beans and mustard greens, pausing occasionally to gaze across the flat rippling fields of the strange land she now calls home.

Mai Vang and her husband Nhia Yang are not ordinary farmers. They are Hmong refugees from Laos—among 105,000 Hmong who have settled in America since they were displaced from their homeland by a nightmare of history.

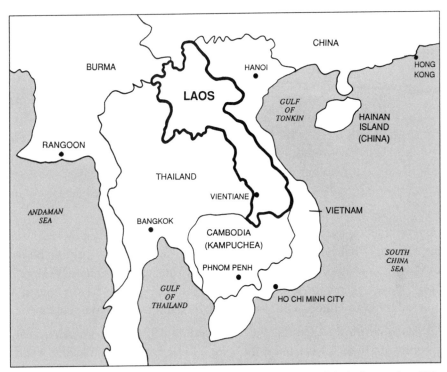

The Hmong are hill tribesmen who lived a peaceful, independent life as seminomadic[1] farmers until the late 1950s when North Vietnam began building the Ho Chi Minh Trail through Laos and Cambodia to carry troops and supplies into South Vietnam.

Many Hmong opposed the North Vietnamese and the communist Pathet Lao forces, allying themselves with the United States and the Royal Lao government. They fought alongside the CIA in a so-called "secret war" against the Pathet Lao and sustained terrible casualties while trying to prevent North Vietnamese troops from marching south.

But when the U.S. pulled out of Vietnam in 1975 and South Vietnam, Cambodia, and Laos fell to the Communists, the Pathet Lao and their Vietnamese allies began attacks on the Hmong. The Pathet Lao newspaper said it was necessary to exterminate the Hmong "to the last root." Former CIA-backed soldiers were hunted down and killed, and whole Hmong villages were gassed or shelled.

Some Hmong were evacuated by the U.S. government, but thousands of others fled on their own to Thailand. And thousands more Hmong still languish in refugee camps, unwanted by the Thai government but facing persecution if they are forced back to Laos.

---

1. seminomadic: having a lifestyle in which people settle homes but move frequently

Mai and Nhia, who was a soldier for more than a decade in the Indochina war, and their oldest child Chang, then 12, escaped in 1975. They gathered up what few possessions they could carry—a cooking pot and some medicinal herbs—and abandoned their land.

They paid a large sum of money for a taxi from their village in Xieng Khouang province to a spot near the Thailand border, with communist soldiers on their tail. They paid another fee that enabled them to hide deep in the jungle for 30 days. After still another payment, they chanced a treacherous predawn crossing of the Mekong River in a wooden boat, praying they would escape the gunfire that had killed so many others on the surging river.

Fortunately, they made it to the relative safety of a refugee camp on the Laotian-Thai border, where they stayed for a year. "I didn't know English," Mai says. "In the camp, they say, 'You sign your name?' I say, 'I don't know.' 'You thirsty?' 'I don't know.'" Then she lapses into the musical tones of Hmong and smiles. Conversation, for the moment, is lost.

Mai, Nhia, and Chang were placed in 1976 with an American sponsor in Ohio. A year later, they joined relatives in Minnesota, where they have fallen back on their age-old farming skills. It is almost as if a Laotian hilltop village were miraculously transported to America.

With their younger children, Pang, 11, and Noel, 12, Mai Vang (Hmong wives retain their personal name) and Nhia Yang and three other families live full-time on 10-acre plots of land in a sort of Hmong farm village. They live in modest dwellings, one family in a cramped mobile home. A fifth family headed by Dang Vang and his wife Ying Yang, both 70, live in an old farmhouse as the village elders on an adjacent cooperative farm.

While the farms supplement their income and provide some food, most of the families have at least two wage earners, a husband and wife working in shifts. Nhia Yang works as a keypunch operator in Minneapolis. Mai Vang lost

Photo by Walter Kale

Mai Vang, husband Nhia Yang, and their children Noel and Pang share dinner at home.

factory and janitorial jobs due to a back problem, and now she does the field work and raises chickens.

They are struggling to maintain some semblance[2] of their lost way of life against the encroachments[3] of a technological society that turns children into Americans very quickly while their parents pine for Laos and worry about the erosion of Hmong values that are based on tight family and clan ties.

In Asia, the Hmong lived apart from society high on mountaintops in misty jungles. Coming to America was their first experience with cities, and it was bewildering. Of all the Southeast Asian refugees, the small, shy, gentle Hmong have had the most difficult adjustment. Most were illiterate in their own language and had never seen indoor plumbing, electricity, telephones, traffic jams, and other staples of modern civilization.

Homesick and depressed, they were preyed on by criminals in the cities and had trouble adjusting to the cold climate. Some of the men began dying mysteriously in their sleep. Psychiatrists tentatively[4] diagnosed the phenomenon as being frightened to death by nightmares, known by its Filipino name of *bangungot*.

Most Hmong men had been soldiers, and after having a lot of responsibility, they had to cope with a lack of status in American society. They didn't know the language and were forced to take the jobs that no one else wanted.

Over the years many Hmong have left the cities for seemingly more hospitable surroundings in rural areas. There are Hmong communities in the foothills of North Carolina, the rain forests of Washington State, the valleys of California, the mountains of western Montana, and the farmlands of Nebraska.

In Minnesota, where more than 15,000 Hmong have settled, 10 cousins pooled their resources—hard-earned money saved from factory or social-service jobs—to purchase a 73-acre farm, the Hiawatha Valley Farm Cooperative, which they cultivate when their city jobs permit.

They grow acres of cucumbers as a cash crop,[5] which they sell to a food-processing company. And they also grow such truck-farm crops[6] as corn, tomatoes, peppers, green beans, onions, lettuce, and squash to sell

---

2. **semblance:** form or likeness
3. **encroachments:** gradual steps into the territory of another
4. **tentatively:** without deciding for certain
5. **cash crop:** any crop produced for sale
6. **truck-farm crops:** vegetables or fruit grown for the market

at farmers markets and to greengrocers. Such Asian herbs as coriander and lemon grass also are grown for their own use and for Oriental restaurateurs. An attempt to grow rice was thwarted[7] by the short Midwestern growing season.

A big white silo marks the site of the farm near Hugo, Minnesota, 25 miles northeast of the Twin Cities. The president of the cooperative is Shoua Vang, a former major in the Lao army who picked up English as a member of special search teams that rescued downed American pilots in the jungles on the Vietnam border by dangling from ropes lowered from helicopters.

Photo by Walter Kale

Pang, Mai Vang, Nhia Yang, and Noel pose in traditional Hmong ceremonial dress.

The Hmong New Year festival, which occurs at the end of November, is one of the most important events in Hmong life. That is when they don exotic traditional garments of bright pink, green, yellow, and red. For women, the costume entails layers of garments and sashes, a silver breastplate necklace, and a headdress. But the most recognizable piece is perhaps the intricate batik-dyed, pleated skirt which may contain as many as 500 tiny individual pleats, depending on its size.

The festive dress of Hmong men is less elaborate: black pants that resemble two identical, equilateral triangles sewn together with openings for the legs and waist, a sash, and a white shirt covered with a vest or black long-sleeved jacket. Headgear can range from an elaborate, festooned cap to a simple one with a pompon.

Hmong women are renowned[8] for their meticulous[9] textile craftsmanship. In Laos they wove and dyed fabrics with natural dyes. They began making needlework for sale in Thai refugee camps, and in America, they are best known for their *pandau,* embroidered story cloths that typically illustrate rural village life.

---

7. **thwarted:** prevented from succeeding
8. **renowned:** famous
9. **meticulous:** very careful of details

Some of the large pieces deal with the great tragedy of the Hmong, depicting military planes, Hmong soldiers fighting the Vietnamese, and the exodus[10] across the Mekong River. Other geometric cloths tell no story, relying instead on pattern, precise appliqué[11] and reverse appliqué, symbols, and detailed stitching for interest.

Hmong mothers traditionally passed on the skills to their daughters, who began embroidery training at an early age. A woman's skill was a source of family pride, and it signaled a girl's readiness for marriage. But now pandau is an endangered art.

Mai Vang holds embroidered cloth.

Photo by Walter Kale

Mai Vang spends the long Minnesota winters embroidering story cloths and making ornaments and counted cross-stitch checkbook covers, all of which she sells along with vegetables from a stall at the Minneapolis farmers market. But her daughter Pang has yet to learn embroidery. Pang says she has been too busy with school and chores and she would like to learn to play the cornet. Few believe the pandau cottage industry will survive in the next generation of American-born Hmong.

The Hmong had no written language until the early 1950s when French and American missionaries working in Laos began to create one. There are 14 vowels in the Hmong language, each with eight tones. Each inflection[12] gives an entirely different meaning to a word.

As new Americans, Hmong refugees are struggling to adjust to a country that could not be more different from their tropical homeland, where the farmland was free and Hmong families frequently moved from place to place. Those in the Minnesota village realize they may never be able to support themselves solely on their farm earnings, but they say that farming keeps them connected to their ancestors.

Their hearts remain in Southeast Asia. "I would like to return to Laos," Nhia Yang says one evening, looking wistfully at the horizon from the back window of his home. "My country is a beautiful country—not hot, not cold. I like my country, but I so scared I not want to stay."

---

10. exodus: departure of a large number of people
11. appliqué: decoration made by attaching one piece of cloth on top of another
12. inflection: change in pitch or tone of voice

"Back to the Land," by Connie Lauerman. From *Chicago Tribune Magazine*, October 1, 1989.

Why is the immigration policy of the United States important to people around the world? The following selection describes trends in the history of United States immigration. Read to discover the challenge in creating a workable and fair immigration policy for the future.

THE CHALLENGE OF IMMIGRATION

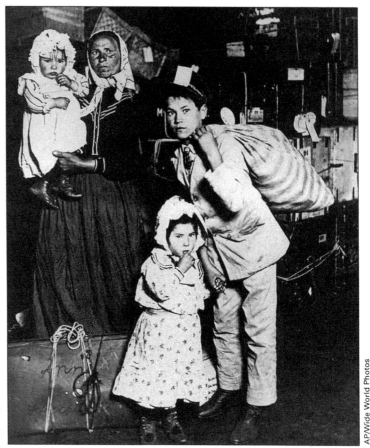

European immigrants on Ellis Island in 1905

It is important that we reflect upon how our country, a nation of immigrants, is addressing the issue of immigration. Our immigration policy is important to people throughout the world, and we have a responsibility to address it forthrightly.[1] The challenge is to develop an approach that will work, that will be fair and humane.

Since the early 1800s, the U.S. has dealt differently with each new wave of immigration. Today, the immigration challenge is posed by millions of people (Mexicans, Latinos, Asians, and others) whose countries are experiencing dire economic problems. It is a situation of enormous complexity and one which this country must face directly and honestly.

First, let's review some of the lessons we have learned as a nation that has absorbed millions of immigrants and has prospered by the energy and talent they brought with them. Generally, immigrants arrived at our eastern shores in large waves, principally from European countries. From the 1840s through the 1860s, Irish, German, and

1. **forthrightly:** directly

English immigrants flocked to the U.S. During the 1870s, the Chinese began streaming to California. Millions of southern and eastern Europeans settled between 1880 and 1920. Each successive influx[2] prompted debate among Americans, who were themselves either former immigrants or the descendants of immigrants. Although many Americans welcomed new immigrants and espoused[3] the Statue of Liberty's poetic scripture to open a "Golden Door," many others wanted to lock the door and throw away the key.

> *"Give me your tired, your poor,*
> *Your huddled masses yearning to breathe free,*
> *The wretched refuse from your teeming shore.*
> *Send these, the homeless, tempest-tost to me,*
> *I lift my lamp beside the golden door!"*

The Bettmann Archive

With each succeeding group of immigrants, our attitudes on acculturation[4] and assimilation[5] changed. During the early years of mass immigration, the concept of assimilation was popular. We believed in America as a melting pot. It was thought best to relinquish one's heritage and to mix into the cultural "mainstream."

Today, there is an increasingly widespread acceptance of the value of preserving one's unique heritage and culture. Many Americans now believe that multicultural understanding and acceptance are important attributes to have in an increasingly complex international environment.

Unfortunately, while there appears to be a growing interest in learning about other cultures and in interacting with other peoples, our government is retrenching[6] from the immigration policies of recent years and is now making it more difficult for people to come to America.

We should not be surprised at this inconsistency, for, contrary to popular belief, we have not always welcomed immigrants. Throughout the periodic battles over immigration policy in our country, opponents of the open door have had more victories than proponents.[7] Time and time again, Congress has passed immigration laws that today can be described as discriminatory. At the turn of the century, Asians characterized as "Mongols" were considered particularly dangerous. We passed a Chinese Exclusion Law in 1882, formed a "Gentlemen's Agreement" with Japan

2. **influx:** flowing in
3. **espoused:** supported
4. **acculturation:** adapting to a different culture
5. **assimilation:** becoming absorbed into the main culture
6. **retrenching:** retreating; going back
7. **proponents:** supporters

in 1907 to halt Japanese immigration, and later created an "Asian Barred Zone" in 1917. Jews, Slavs, and Italians were also considered racially or culturally inferior, so Congress passed national origin quotas in 1921 and 1924. The quotas were designed to freeze the ethnic composition of our population by limiting entrance of any one nationality to a small percentage. Eventually, we placed a ceiling of 150,000 immigrants who could come from outside the Western Hemisphere. These ceilings included almost everyone except northern Europeans, Canadians, and, interestingly, Mexicans, who were needed as farm workers. Nevertheless, millions of people immigrated to America, raised families, prospered, and became citizens.

The Changing Face of Immigration

Now we, the children of immigrants, are witnessing yet another major influx of people from throughout the world. This time, however, the nationalities are different. Today, roughly 80 percent of all immigrants come from Latin America and Asia. Unlike immigrant groups which preceded them, their first impression of their new home is likely to be shaped by the skyline of Los Angeles, not the majestic Statue of Liberty. By the year 2080, as many as 37 percent of all Americans could be descended from someone who came to this country after 1980. Unquestionably, these trends will have a substantial impact on the U.S. as we know it today.

The backgrounds of immigrants are very different today, and so are their numbers. For example, during the 1970s, our nation absorbed about 4,500,000 legal immigrants. An estimated 3,500,000 undocumented workers sought employment here as well. In this decade, the pace of immigration will likely accelerate. We have yet to feel the impact of additional immigration driven by the 1986 earthquake and rapid decline of oil prices in Mexico. If Mexico does not receive support to ease its $96 billion trade deficit and to help stabilize its economy, we can expect even more people to come north in the hope of finding economic security.

As was the case early in our nation's history, many officials are claiming that new immigrants will hurt America. However, we have learned a lot from the hysteria of the past. In fact, recent studies are challenging the assertion that immigrants are a drain on our economy.

Courtney Slater, former chief economist in the Commerce Department, has found that undocumented workers have been a big factor in the job market in many communities and that their impact has been more beneficial than we might think. Her analysis, presented in *American Demographics Magazine* (January 1985), concluded that the concentration of low-wage labor provided by undocumented workers helped attract industries to certain cities. With more industries moving into an area, competition among businesses resulted in lower consumer prices and an actual increase in total employment. She also found that undocumented workers did not take jobs away from Americans. Slater concluded that their willingness to accept low-paying jobs may, in some areas, hold down wages, but that was balanced against the positive effect of additional jobs generated by more competitive industries and the resulting lower costs of products to consumers.

There are other studies demonstrating that immigrants have a positive effect on the American economy, but some policymakers would have us believe that the U.S. is under siege. They make sensational claims that our nation is "losing control of its borders" or that we are in danger of becoming a "Hispanic Quebec."[8]

Inflammatory rhetoric[9] of this sort should alarm all Americans. It certainly frightens Hispanic-Americans whose roots in America are centuries old. For Hispanics whose sons and daughters have earned hundreds of medals of honor in defending our country, real anger is growing over slurs which impugn[10] their loyalty, patriotism, or integrity. Hispanic-Americans are concerned that proposed immigration legislation will foster anti-Hispanic feelings that will eventually be directed at native-born Americans.

All Americans—whether of European, Asian, or Hispanic descent—are concerned about our nation's immigration practices. We know that neither emotional rhetoric nor simplistic, knee-jerk solutions will solve the challenging problem of immigration. We should, therefore, learn from our past mistakes

---

8. Quebec: province in Canada where the French-speaking culture seeks to remain separate from the nation's larger English-speaking culture.

9. inflammatory rhetoric: words likely to stir anger

10. impugn: challenge as being false; question

and use our creative and entrepreneurial[11] skills to fashion new approaches to this complicated socio-political issue. We should focus on the causes of immigration, not its symptoms. As we have learned from the field of medicine, prevention of illness by addressing its cause is more sensible and cost-effective than last-minute surgery.

Meeting the Challenge

A solution to the immigration challenge starts by recognizing that the causes of immigration pressures are primarily economic. The disparities[12] between the U.S. and South and Central American countries are enormous. If one examines the inflation rates and the foreign debts facing Latin American countries, one begins to understand their desperation. Put simply, people in Mexico and Central America are hard-pressed to survive in their countries due to their dismal economic conditions.

Secondly, let us recognize that Mexico ranks third among our trading partners. From a geopolitical standpoint, Mexico is an ally and a neighbor which shares kinship with millions of Americans. It makes good, common sense to work with Mexico in a cooperative effort to address immigration issues. It is in our best interest to develop joint solutions without violating the civil and human rights of Mexican and American citizens.

We need new ideas for immigration reform; the old ones have failed. We need new approaches that address the *causes* of immigration, not old remedies that focus on its *symptoms*.

The problem of immigrants and refugees from Central America, Vietnam, Haiti, and other troubled spots around the globe are equally complex. The U.S. needs to analyze the factors of our foreign policy that might contribute to the flight of individuals from their home countries.

What is abundantly clear is that the history of immigration control has been inconsistently applied. It is time that we recognize that there are no easy answers to this problem and that it will not be resolved through simplistic measures. We must come to understand the reasons for the immigration surge in all their complexity. We must be willing to develop comprehensive,[13] innovative approaches to solving these problems and, as always, must be vigilant[14] against the rhetoric of ignorance that can only divide a nation whose unique heritage is its pride in its diversity.

11. **entrepreneurial skills:** skills in business organization and management
12. **disparities:** inequalities
13. **comprehensive:** large in scope
14. **vigilant:** watchful

"The Challenge of Immigration," by Fredrico Pena. Reprinted from *USA Today Magazine*, January copyright 1987 by the Society for the Advancement of Education.

Unit 3: Political Science

the study of how governments work

THE COUNTY ELECTION, 1851/52, George Caleb Bingham, American, 1811-1879
The Saint Louis Art Museum

What dangers exist when one person or group holds all the power in a government? Read to learn about the system our nation's founders set up to control the power of the federal government.

The Capitol Building

Ted Russell/The Image Bank

Santi Visalli/The Image Bank

The White House

THE CHECKS AND BALANCE SYSTEM

The Supreme Court

Marc Romanelli/The Image Bank

The framers[1] of the Constitution wanted to make sure that the people's rights would always be safe and that the central or federal government would never become too powerful. A government to work most efficiently and democratically ought to have three major powers: to make laws, to carry out those laws, and to provide justice under law for the best interests of the people. Should these three functions be in the hands of one person or one group, there would be great danger that that person or group could use the power for personal profit rather than for the people. To guard against this possibility, the Constitution provided for three major branches of government: the legislature, or Congress, to make laws; the executive to carry out the laws; and the judiciary to watch over

1. **framers:** authors

the rights of the people as described in the Constitution.

The powers of these three branches of the government are described carefully in the Constitution. The men of 1787 were so afraid of too much power in the hands of a few that they worked hard and long to spell out each job for the three parts of the federal government. Nothing was to be left to chance. To make sure that the government should never take more power than what it was granted in the Constitution, it was carefully stated that any power not given to the government should forever belong to the states. This remarkably foresighted decision meant that, although the country could grow from a little one into a great nation over the years, the rights of the people could never be absorbed by the federal government. If changing times cause new problems to arise, the states or the people have the right to decide what to do. No one branch of the federal government can simply assume the power and not answer to the people.

Another reason for describing carefully the powers of the three branches was to prevent any one branch from becoming stronger than the others. Each job in the running of the country was balanced between the legislative, the executive, and the judicial branches. The jobs were also intertwined. Each part of the government can only function in relation to the others. This system not only balances power between the three branches, but also provides a check on each branch by the others. For instance, a good example of the check system can be found in the manner in which laws become laws. The legislature, or

Congress, has the job of drafting[2] laws for the country. Once a bill, as a law is called before it is signed by the president, has been passed[3] by the two houses, the Senate and the House of Representatives, the Congress must send a copy to the chief executive, the president of the United States, for his approval. He then has four options as to what he may do. He may agree with the bill and sign the copy, in which case the law goes into effect. Or, if he should feel that it is not a good law, he may veto it. Vetoing means that he refuses to sign. Should he do that, the copy is returned to the house of Congress in which it originated. If the Congress, sure that the proposed law is a necessary one, passes it again by a two-thirds majority, the bill becomes law regardless of the president's veto. The people are represented in Congress, and if they still favor the law, it is more democratic that they should have it. The foresighted writers of the Constitution saw that there would be times when the people could disagree with the president, and should this occur, the people in a democracy should have the last word. This is the meaning of democracy. There are also two other possibilities open to the president in the making of a law. He may ignore the bill and allow it to lie on his desk for 10 days, excluding Sundays. Should he do this, he indicates his disapproval, but he does not veto it. After 10 days that act becomes law, provided that Congress is in session. This course of action gives the president a chance to register an opinion between yes and no, and at

2. drafting: writing
3. passed: approved by vote

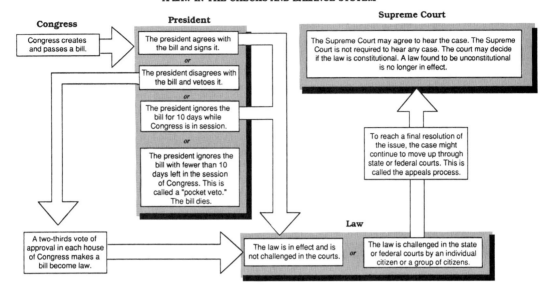

A LAW IN THE CHECKS AND BALANCE SYSTEM

Congress

Congress creates and passes a bill.

President

The president agrees with the bill and signs it.

or

The president disagrees with the bill and vetoes it.

or

The president ignores the bill for 10 days while Congress is in session.

or

The president ignores the bill with fewer than 10 days left in the session of Congress. This is called a "pocket veto." The bill dies.

Supreme Court

The Supreme Court may agree to hear the case. The Supreme Court is not required to hear any case. The court may decide if the law is constitutional. A law found to be unconstitutional is no longer in effect.

To reach a final resolution of the issue, the case might continue to move up through state or federal courts. This is called the appeals process.

A two-thirds vote of approval in each house of Congress makes a bill become law.

Law

The law is in effect and is not challenged in the courts.

or

The law is challenged in the state or federal courts by an individual citizen or a group of citizens.

times it is very important that he should have the opportunity of saying nothing instead of being forced to agree or disagree. His fourth option is to exercise what is called the "pocket veto." This means that if a bill comes to him and there are fewer than 10 days remaining in the congressional session, the president may decide to leave it unsigned, and it automatically dies. Should the people through Congress still wish to enact the law, it must be reintroduced in the next legislative session, and the whole process begins anew.

The checks system goes further. The judicial branch has its say about the laws of the land. Once the Congress and the president have agreed upon a law, it must be enforced all over the United States. Should someone disagree with a federal law and challenge it by disobeying it, the case is brought into the court system of the United States. If the Supreme Court should decide to hear a case, it has the duty of examining the law and determining if it is constitutional, or, in other words, whether the law is in keeping with the rights of the people as outlined in the Constitution. It should be noted, however, that the right of judicial review, as this practice is called, is not stated as such in the Constitution. It became an enduring part of the checks and balance system as early as 1803 through an interpretation of the Constitution by Chief Justice John Marshall in the famous case of *Marbury* v. *Madison.*

This system of balanced power and of checks between the branches of the government reflects the political genius of the Founding Fathers. It has meant that at all times the people's rights and interests are being carefully guarded.

There is virtually no chance that a strong man or a group of men can take over the government and force the rest of the people to do their will. It must be stressed, however, that as Jefferson said, "Eternal vigilance[4] is the price of liberty," and if the people of the United States, their elected representatives, and their judges are not constantly vigilant, no mere words on paper are going to protect their freedom.

---

4. eternal vigilance: unending watchfulness to danger or trouble

From *Our Federal Government and How It Works,* by Patricia C. Acheson.

How would you feel about deciding if someone were guilty or innocent of a crime? The following selection describes the importance of the jury in America and how it works. As you read, consider how much power the members of a jury hold.

View of a trial from the jury box. Jurors are seated at left.

The Jury System IN America

By far the most successful migration of the English model jury was across the Atlantic. While in New England, the colonists of the seventeenth century generally did not feel bound by English common law[1]—they had suffered too much from governmental tyranny for that—they did adopt the English concepts of property, liberty, and justice to the extent they considered them appropriate for a new life in a new land. The jury system was certainly one way for a people seeking freedom to curb the authority of the state. In the European countries, the jury system was grafted[2] onto a tree of existing legal traditions. In some cases the graft did not take at all, and the new limb eventually dropped off; in other cases, it shrank considerably in size. In the American

---

1. **common law:** law based on custom and past court decisions rather than written and enacted law
2. **grafted:** joined

colonies, however, the jury system was an integral part of the Tree of Liberty that was planted at the time of our nation's birth. As such, it has flourished here as it has nowhere else in the world.

Today at least 80 percent of all criminal jury trials worldwide take place in the United States. Not only is the system most deeply rooted here and most thoroughly accepted, but it also gives jurors more power—that is, more freedom of decision—than they are allowed in any other major nation. This power is simply the reverse side of the coin of responsibility, and in the United States the responsibility for achieving justice, like all other aspects of government, is derived from and rests with the people. The principle is so important to us that the right to trial by jury is preserved in our Constitution in both Article 3 and in the Sixth Amendment of the Bill of Rights, and it is guaranteed in every state constitution as well. Aside from voting in elections, where the impact of any one person's choice is weakened by the huge number of voters in the group, the jury system allows individuals more direct and effective expression of their will than any other institution we now have. Writing letters to congressmen, marching on the Pentagon, handing out leaflets on a street corner near the White House, and demonstrating in front of City Hall are all valid ways for us to make our views known and to influence the men and women we have elected to govern us. Such measures, however dramatic they may be, may or may not change anything. But the verdict of 12 people sitting in a small-town courthouse in Wyoming, having heard a case that is unpublicized and unknown outside of the community, may restore a man to his family or may take him from that family forever.

Why is the power, and the responsibility, of jurors greater in the United States than anywhere else? The jury system came to the United States with the first English colonists, but it responded to and was shaped by what is distinctly the American experience. From Westerns we all know about the "frontier justice" practiced by people living in settlements with only the beginnings of an organized legal system, or perhaps with none at all, who regularly "took the law into their own hands" and punished a presumed offender in whatever manner they saw fit. They couldn't wait for the judge who rode into town once every few months or so. Besides, they didn't necessarily trust that judge anyway.

There is in the American character a fundamental distrust or at least a suspicion of authority. Political leaders tend to be most revered after they have died or left office. And if in an increasingly complex society, ordinary people recognize that they must give to others ever greater control over their own daily lives, they are all the more apt to cherish and keep for themselves whatever power they legitimately can. One of the last strongholds of such power is in the jury box. There, average citizens, having no special qualifications of any kind, actively participate in the workings of one of the three chief branches of government, the judicial system. They can freely exercise their own judgment, and, to a truly extraordinary extent, they can still take the law into their own hands.

In other countries trial power is divided between judges and jurors, with the former required to give strong direction to the deliberations[3] of the latter. In United States criminal courts, there is not so much a sharing of power as a division of powers. The judge is supreme in determining how a trial is to proceed and what evidence will be permitted. The jury is supreme in determining the guilt or innocence of the accused. In this regard, the guidance jurors receive from a judge is minimal. While in most states a judge in his final charge[4] to the jury is permitted to review and summarize the evidence that has been presented during the trial, in some states he may not even do that. In his charge, his authority is limited to instructing the jurors on the law in question and explaining the counts on which the defendant[5] has been indicted.[6] But the fact is that, in either case, after they have retired to the jury room to deliberate, the jurors may in effect choose to ignore—indeed, to defy—everything they have just been told.

To illustrate, let's imagine that in his charge a judge has gone into considerable detail in outlining a state law that prohibits most forms of gambling. While he has not discussed why the statute was passed, he has stressed that at this time and place it is beyond the jurors' function to question the wisdom of their state legislators in enacting such a law: it is "on the books" and therefore must be enforced. If the jury believes that the defendant has, as charged, broken this law by setting up and managing an illegal betting establishment, they must, the judge declares, find him guilty. Upon retiring to the jury room, the jurors begin their deliberations and all quickly agree that the defendant did in fact operate a betting parlor. He is then clearly guilty.

"But wait," says one juror. "Sure, this guy was running the bookie joint, but it was never absolutely proved that he owned it." When only

---

3. **deliberations:** discussions before reaching a decision
4. **charge:** giving of instructions
5. **defendant:** person accused of a crime
6. **indicted:** formally accused

two other jurors express doubt on this point, the first juror is forced to admit what really troubles him. "Okay," he says, "let's say he does own the place. So what? What real harm was the poor guy doing when he let those people place their lousy two buck bets?"

"Right!" says someone else, and in time all of the jurors conclude that the defendant was probably doing no great harm to anyone.

"Then why the hell convict him?" asks the first gadfly[7] of a juror.

"Well, he did break the law," another juror remarks rather timidly.

"Sure," says the first juror, "but what about the guy who can take the day off to go to the track with 2000 bucks that his family really needs? He drops all of it by the last race and comes home without a dime. Does he get arrested? No, it's all perfectly legal."

Thus the jury has come upon an entirely new path, one that the judge certainly never intended these 12 people to follow—and, with some help from that vague doubt about the ownership of the betting parlor, the path leads almost inevitably to a verdict of not guilty.

SOME GUIDELINES FOR JURORS ON REACHING A DECISION

❏ Jurors must be patient and careful not to form conclusions until they have heard all of the evidence and argument and have received the instructions of the court on the law.

❏ Generally, one who asserts a claim must prove that claim to your satisfaction by a fair preponderance of the credible evidence.

❏ You should not discuss the case with anyone, nor permit any person to speak to you about it, until the case is finally submitted to you for decision, and then speak only with your fellow jurors in the case.

❏ Sympathy, prejudice, or bias should play no part in a verdict by an American jury.

❏ If you do not keep an open mind until the case is finally submitted to you, it may result in a snap judgment, in much disagreeable wrangling in the jury room, and in an injustice to the parties involved.

❏ In deciding a case, you are only expected to apply the same common sense that you use in the conduct of your daily affairs.

❏ Be courteous to and patient with your fellow jurors. If you listen, without stubbornness, to the discussions by the others in the jury room and can harmonize conflicting views, you will generally reach a sound verdict.

From *A Handbook for Trial Jurors of Broome County* (State of New York)

---

7. **gadfly:** person who stirs up others

Burning draft cards

Obviously, juries do not very often effectively repeal a law passed by a democratically elected legislature. But in what are sometimes called "political trials"—where the defendant's views on a controversial public issue assume an importance at least equal to the matter of his or her guilt—jury nullification[8] of the law is not at all uncommon. During the Vietnam War, for example, men and women charged with destroying government property as part of their antiwar demonstrations were acquitted[9] even though their burning of draft board records was beyond question. That jurors, in the face of decisive evidence to the contrary, should render not-guilty verdicts is a stunning commentary on the jury system. Whether that commentary is favorable or unfavorable is in itself a highly controversial issue among judges, attorneys, and students of the law. For the moment, we must simply marvel at the power that 12 ordinary people—strangers to one another and engaged in no conspiracy,[10] not elected to any sort of office, and not educated in the ways of the law—can, under the right circumstances, command.

---

8. **nullification:** making useless
9. **acquitted:** cleared of a charge
10. **conspiracy:** secret plot with a harmful purpose

From *Beyond a Reasonable Doubt,* by Melvyn Zerman.

Were you counted in the 1990 census? The United States Constitution requires that a census be taken every 10 years. Read to discover the history of the census and how it is used to give citizens an equal voice in government.

The Evolution of One Person, One Vote

Every decade for the last 200 years, Americans have complied with the Constitution and counted themselves. But since the first enumeration[1] of the American people in 1790, the census has been more than a head count of the growing country. It's been an indicator of the evolution of American political values.

On its simplest level, the census is a means to document historical changes in the American population. But since it determines how federal funds, power, and political clout are divided among the American people, the census often serves as a vehicle for social change.

Proof of Importance

When the country's first census was taken in 1790, Americans waited anxiously for the results. As a newly independent nation, the United States was proud, and wanted to show the world that it was a populous and important place.

Marshals[2] of the first census faced a difficult task. In many parts of the country, roads were poor or nonexistent, boundaries were uncertain, the population was scattered, and people were suspicious of strangers prying into their private lives. President George Washington warned the country that the combination of these factors would probably produce a significant undercount of the nation's actual population.

The first census recorded fewer than the four million to five million

1. **enumeration:** counting
2. **marshals:** federal officials appointed to conduct the census

Americans the public expected it to uncover, but it documented a diversity of names that helped forge America's reputation as the world's melting pot. Among the 3,929,214 people it counted were Truelove Sparks, Booze Still, Wanton Bump, and Boston Frog. And the first census recorded 27,337 different family names, including Cusser, Dunce, Hungerpealer, Pettyfool, and Madsavage.

White Rights

Despite all these different names, the first census reflected the political reality of the new nation as a place where the rights of white men were put above those of everyone else. Only male heads of households were asked to supply information to the census. Each man was asked about the number of women and children in *his* household. White slave owners supplied census takers with inventories of their "human property." And no attempt was made to count Native Americans, other than the few who had joined white society and were paying taxes.

Population Boom

For 70 years, the census was conducted in much the same manner. Any fears the young country had about not appearing important to European powers were erased by the nation's rapid growth, which the census documented each decade. From 1790 to 1869, the population boomed from under four million to over 31 million.

In response to the growth of the population, the number of representatives to the House of Representatives increased from 105 after the 1790 census

to 241 after the 1860 census. During the same period, the nation's slave population swelled from under 700,000 to nearly four million. And during that period, on the census, and in the eyes of the law, slaves were counted as 3/5—only 60 percent—of a person. The outcome of the Civil War (1861–65) put an end to that practice.

Social Change

By 1870, the North had won the war, Abraham Lincoln had outlawed slavery, and the 14th Amendment to the Constitution finally empowered blacks to participate in politics. The 1870 census was more than a tabulation[3] of postwar America. It was an instrument of social change. It helped cement the political influence of black Americans by determining the numbers of potential black voters, and ensuring that all, not a fraction, of black Americans were represented in Congress.

It took two more decades before the census finally included Native Americans. Until 1890, they were largely ignored by the census. Enumerators were instructed not to count "Indians roaming individually, or in bands, over unsettled tracts of country."

But by 1890, the last of America's western frontier was inhabited by white settlers. American Indians could no longer be considered a separate nation living in North America. And nearly every American Indian had either been killed in battle, wiped out by white diseases, or moved by force onto reservations under the authority of the U.S. government.

---

3. **tabulation:** arrangement of data

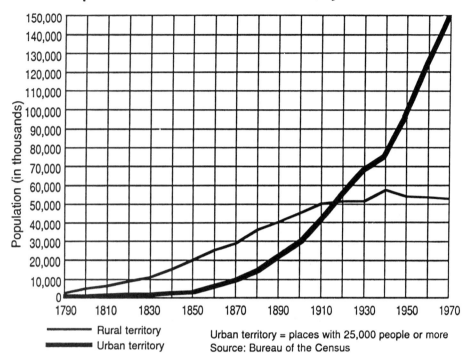

Population in Urban and Rural Territory: 1790 to 1970

Population (in thousands)

——— Rural territory
━━━ Urban territory

Urban territory = places with 25,000 people or more
Source: Bureau of the Census

The 1890 census accepted the fact that Indians had become "part of the ordinary population of the country," and directed that "they be embraced in the enumeration, and represented in Congress."

During the first two decades of the 20th century, European immigrants poured into American cities. By 1920, the census revealed that 106 million Americans—51 percent of the population—lived in and around cities. For the first time, the nation's urban population had become greater than the rural population. The results of the 1920 census meant that the large urban states of the Northeast and Midwest stood to gain the most seats in the House and the most clout in Congress.

The Rural Revolt

But congressional leaders from rural areas refused to surrender political power to the large urban states. They argued that geography was the true basis for representation, and said that urban states did not deserve more representation for their foreign-born residents. The rural revolt succeeded, and for the first time in the country's history, Congress refused to redistribute seats in the House based on the census figures.

Finally in 1929, Congress passed a reapportionment[4] bill based on the results of the 1930 census. But as part of a difficult compromise worked out with the rebellious rural lawmakers, Congress

---

4. reapportionment: redistribution of the number of seats in the legislature among areas represented

removed the existing requirements for equal-sized congressional districts.

Until the 1960s, congressional districts in large urban areas often encompassed[5] seven or eight times as many people as rural congressional districts. In practice, that meant that rural America was still able to control Congress.

One Person, One Vote

In 1962, 175 years after our Founding Fathers set the census in motion, the Supreme Court, in a landmark[6] decision, made equal representation for every American the law of the land. In his impassioned ruling on *Baker* v. *Carr,* Chief Justice Earl Warren declared unequal congressional districts unconstitutional. "Legislators represent people," Warren explained in his majority opinion, "not trees or acres. Legislators are elected by voters, not farms, or cities, or economic interests."

A person casts his vote by pulling a lever in a voting booth.

By the late 1960s, congressional districts around the country were redrawn to meet the court's call for equal representation. And after the 1970 census, underrepresented urban areas were finally given an equal voice in Congress. Today, the census still undercounts minorities. But the country is closer than ever to the ideal of "one man, one vote" that motivated the Founding Fathers to establish the census more than 200 years ago.

---

5. **encompassed:** contained
6. **landmark:** event of historic importance

"The Evolution of One Person, One Vote," by David Oliver Relin. From *Scholastic Update,* January 12, 1990.

Unit 4: Behavioral Science

the study of why people act and feel the way they do

MARISOL, SELF PORTRAIT, 1961-62, Marisol Escobar
Museum of Contemporary Art, Promised gift of Joseph and Jory Shapiro

Do you believe the American family was stronger in the past? The following selection examines changes in American family life. As you read, consider what the future may hold for the American family.

JANEART LTD./The Image Bank

Nick Pavloff/The Image Bank

Sobel/Kolosky/The Image Bank

Elyse Lewin/The Image Bank

WHAT HAPPENED TO THE FAMILY?

The American family does not exist. Rather, we are creating many American families, of diverse styles and shapes. In unprecedented[1] numbers, our families are unalike: we have fathers working while mothers keep house; fathers and mothers both working away from home; single parents; second marriages bringing children together from unrelated backgrounds; childless couples; unmarried couples, with and without children; gay and lesbian parents. We are living through a period of historic change in American family life.

The upheaval is evident everywhere in our culture. Babies have babies, kids refuse to grow up and leave home, affluent Yuppies[2] prize their BMWs more than children, rich and poor children alike blot their minds with drugs, people casually move in with each other and out again. The divorce rate has doubled since 1965, and demographers project that half of all first marriages today will end in divorce. Six out of 10 second marriages will prob-

---

1. **unprecedented:** not seen before
2. **Yuppies:** young, college-educated adults who have good jobs and work near or in a big city

Families Below Poverty Level in 1987

All Families
12.1 %

White Families
10.5 %

Black Families
33.1 %

Families with Female
Householder, No
Husband Present
33.6 %

Source: U.S. Bureau of the Census

ably collapse. One third of all children born in the past decade will probably live in a stepfamily before they are 18. One out of every four children today is being raised by a single parent. About 22 percent of children today were born out of wedlock; of those, about a third were born to a teenage mother. One out of every five children lives in poverty; the rate is twice as high among blacks and Hispanics.

Most of us are still reeling from the shock of such turmoil. Americans—in their living rooms, in their boardrooms, and in the halls of Congress—are struggling to understand what has gone wrong. We find family life worse than it was a decade ago, according to a *Newsweek* poll, and we are not sanguine[3] about the next decade. For instance, two thirds of those polled think a family should be prepared to make "financial sacrifices so that one parent can stay home to raise the children." But that isn't likely to happen. An astonishing two-thirds of all mothers are in the labor force, roughly double the rate in 1955, and more than half of all mothers of infants are in the work force.

Parents feel torn between work and family obligations. Marriage is a fragile institution—not something anyone can count on. Children seem to be paying the price for their elders' confusion. "There is an increasing understanding of the emotional cost of having children," says Larry L. Bumpass, a University of Wisconsin demographer. "People once thought parenting ended when their children were 18. Now they know it stretches into the 20s and beyond." Divorce has left a devastated generation in its wake, and for many youngsters, the pain is compounded by poverty and neglect. While politicians and psychologists debate cause and solution, everyone suffers. Even the most traditional of families feel an uneasy sense of emotional dislocation. Three decades ago the mother who kept the house spotless and cooked dinner for her husband and children each evening could be confident and secure in her role. Today, although her numbers are still strong—a third of mothers whose children are under 18 stay home—the woman who opts out of a paycheck may well feel defensive, undervalued, as though she were too incompetent to get "a real job." And yet the traditional family retains a profound hold on the American imagination.

---

3. **sanguine:** hopeful; optimistic

The historical irony[4] here is that the traditional family is something of an anomaly.[5] From Colonial days to the mid-19th century, most fathers and mothers worked side by side, in or near their homes, farming or plying trades. Each contributed to family income, and—within carefully delineated[6] roles—they shared the responsibility of child rearing. Only with the advent of the Industrial Revolution[7] did men go off to work in a distant place like a factory or an office. Men alone began producing the family income; by being away from home much of the time, however, they also surrendered much of their influence on their children. Mothers, who by social custom weren't supposed to work for pay outside the home, minded the hearth, nurtured the children, and placed their economic well-being totally in the hands of their husbands.

Most scholars now consider the "breadwinner-homemaker" model unusual, applicable in limited circumstances for a limited time. It was a distinctly white middle-class phenomenon, for example; it never applied widely among blacks or new immigrants, who could rarely afford to have only a single earner in the family. This model thrived roughly from 1860 to 1920, peaking, as far as demographers can measure, about 1890. Demographers and historians see no dramatic turning point just then, but rather a confluence[8] of social and economic circumstances. Husbands' absolute control of family finances and their independent lives away from home shook the family structure. A long recession beginning in 1893 strained family finances. At the same time, new attention was being paid to women's education. Around this period, the Census Bureau captured a slow, steady parallel climb in the rates of working women and divorce—a climb that has shown few signs of slowing down throughout this century.

The years immediately after World War II, however, seemed to mark a reaffirmation of the traditional family. The return of the soldiers led directly to high fertility rates and the famous baby boom. The median age of first marriage, which had been climbing for decades, fell in 1956 to a historic low, 22.5 years for men and 20.1 for women. The divorce rate slumped slightly. Women, suddenly more likely to be married and to have children, were also satisfied to give up the jobs they had held in record numbers during the war. A general prosperity made it possible for men alone to support their families. Then, by the early '60s, all those developments, caused by aberrational[9] postwar conditions, reverted to the patterns they had followed throughout the century. The fertility rate went down, and the age of first marriage went back up. Prosperity cycled to recession, and the divorce rate again rose and women plunged back heartily into the job market. In 1960, 19 percent of mothers with children under six were in the work force, along with 39 percent of those with children between six and 17. Thus, while the Cleaver family and Ozzie and Harriet were still planting

---

4. **irony:** inconsistency between what is expected and what actually occurs
5. **anomaly:** something unusual
6. **delineated:** defined
7. **Industrial Revolution:** time of great social and economic change resulting from the introduction of power-driven machines and the growth of factories
8. **confluence:** coming together
9. **aberrational:** not typical

the idealized family deeper into the national subconscious, it was struggling.

Now the tradition survives, in a way, precisely because of Ozzie and Harriet. The television programs of the '50s and '60s validated a family style during a period in which today's leaders— congressmen, corporate executives, university professors, magazine editors—were growing up or beginning to establish their own families. (The impact of the idealized family was further magnified by the very size of the postwar generation.) "The traditional model reaches back as far as personal memory goes for most of those who [currently] teach and write and philosophize," says Yale University historian John Demos. "And in a time when parents seem to feel a great deal of change in family experience, that image is comfortingly solid and secure, a counterpoint[10] to what we think is threatening for the future."

We *do* feel uneasy about the future. We have just begun to admit that exchanging old-fashioned family values for independence and self-expression may exact a price. "This is an incendiary[11] issue," says Arlie Hochschild, a sociologist at the University of California, Berkeley, and author of the controversial book *The Second Shift*. "Husbands, wives, children are not getting enough family

'61 PONTIAC, Bechtle, Robert b. 1932,
Collection of Whitney Museum of American Art, New York

life. Nobody is. People are hurting." A mother may go to work because her family needs the money, or to afford luxuries, or because she is educated for a career or because she wants to; she will be more independent but she will probably see less of her children. And her husband, if she has a husband, is not likely to make up the difference with the children. We want it both ways.

We're glad we live in a society that is more comfortable living with gay couples, working women, divorced men, and stepparents and single mothers— people who are reaching in some fashion for self-fulfillment. But we also understand the value of a family life that will provide a stable and nurturing environment in which to raise children— in other words, an environment in which personal goals have to be sacrificed. How do we reconcile the two?

10. counterpoint: contrast
11. incendiary: stirring up conflict

The answer lies in some hard thinking about what a family is for. What do we talk about when we talk about family? Many of us have an emotional reaction to that question. Thinking about family reminds us of the way we were, and the way we dreamed we might be. We remember trips in the car, eager to find out whose side of the road would have more cows and horses to count. We remember raking leaves and the sound of a marching band at the high-school football game. We remember doing homework and wondering what college might be like. It was not all fun and games, of course. There were angry words spoken, and parents and grandparents who somehow were no longer around, and for some of us not enough to eat or clothes not warm enough or nice enough. Then we grow up and marvel at what we can accomplish, and the human beings we can produce, and we sometimes doubt our ability to do the things we want to do—have to do—for our children. And live our own lives besides.

Practical considerations require us to pin down what the family is all about. Tax bills, welfare and insurance payments, adoption rights, and other real-life events can turn on what constitutes a family. Our expectations of what a family ought to be will also shape the kinds of social policies we want. Webster's offers 22 definitions. The Census Bureau has settled on "two or more persons related by birth, marriage or adoption who reside in the same household."

A State of California task force on the future of the family came up with still another conclusion. It decided a family could be measured by the things it should do for its members, which it called "functions": maintain the physical health and safety of its members; help shape a belief system of goals and values; teach social skills; and create a place for recuperation from external stresses. In a recent "family values" survey conducted for the Massachusetts Mutual Insurance Co., respondents were given several choices of family definitions; three quarters of them chose "a group who love and care for each other." Ultimately, to appropriate U.S. Supreme Court Justice Potter Stewart's memorable dictum,[12] we may not be able to define a family, but we know one when we see it.

We enter the 21st century with a heightened sensitivity to family issues. Helping parents and children is a bottom-line concern, no longer a matter of debate. Economists say the smaller labor force of the future means that every skilled employee will be an increasingly valuable asset; we won't be able to afford to waste human resources. Even now companies cannot ignore the needs of working parents. Support systems like day care are becoming a necessity. High rates of child poverty and child abuse are everybody's problem, as is declining school performance and anything else that threatens our global competitiveness. "By the end of the century," says Columbia University sociologist Sheila B. Kamerman, "it will be conventional wisdom to invest in our children."

Those are the familiar demographic[13] forces. But there are other potential tremors just below the surface. By 2020, one in three children will come from a

---

12. **dictum:** statement or saying
13. **demographic:** dealing with the characteristics of the population

Nursing care center

Day care center

minority group—Hispanic-Americans, African-Americans, Asian-Americans, and others. Their parents will command unprecedented political clout. Minorities and women together will make up the majority of new entrants into the work force. Minority children are usually the neediest among us, and they will want government support, especially in the schools. At about the same time, many baby boomers will be retired, and they will want help from Washington as well. Billions of dollars are at stake, and the country's priorities in handing out those dollars are not yet clear. After all, children and the elderly are both part of our families. How should the government spend taxpayers' dollars— on long-term nursing care or better day care?

So far, the political debate on family issues has split largely along predictable ideological lines. Conservatives want to preserve the family of the '50s; they say there has been too much governmental intrusion already, with disastrous results. Their evidence: the underclass, a veritable caste of untouchables[14] in the inner cities where the cycle of welfare dependency and teenage pregnancy thwarts attempts at reform. Liberals say government can and should help. We can measure which

programs work, they say; we just don't put our money and support in the right places. Enrichment programs like Head Start, better prenatal[15] care, quality day care—no one questions the effectiveness of these efforts. And liberals see even more to be done. "We have a rare opportunity to make changes now that could be meaningful into the next century," says Marian Wright Edelman, president of the Children's Defense Fund. But many elements that liberals would like to see on a children's agenda are certain to generate bitter political controversy. Among some of the things that could be included in a national family policy:

- Child and family allowances with payments scaled to the number of children in each family;
- Guarantees to mothers of full job protection, seniority, and benefits upon their return to work after maternity leave;
- Pay equity for working women;
- Cash payments to mothers for wages lost during maternity leave;
- Full health-care programs for all children;
- National standards for day care.

---

14. caste of untouchables: term once used for the social class with the lowest ranking in the society of India. The touch of people in this group was considered unclean for those in higher social classes.
15. prenatal: before birth

Our legacy to the future must be a program of action that transcends ideology.[16] And there are indications that we are watching the birth of a liberal/conservative coalition[17] on family issues. "Family issues ring true for people across the political spectrum," says David Blankenhorn, president of the Institute for American Values, a New York think tank[18] on family policy issues. "The well-being of families is both politically and culturally resonant;[19] it is something that touches people's everyday lives." The government is already responding to the challenge in some ways. For example, President George Bush agreed at the 1989 Education Summit to support increased funding for Head Start, which is by common consent the most successful federal program for preschoolers, yet in 1989 reached only 18 percent of the eligible children.

These issues will occupy us on a national level well into the next century. Yet in our everyday lives, we have begun to find solutions. Some mothers, torn between a desire to stay home with their children and to move ahead in their careers, are adopting a style known as sequencing. After establishing themselves in their career or earning an advanced degree, they step off the career ladder for a few years to focus on children and home. When children reach school age, they return to full-time jobs. Others take a less drastic approach, temporarily switching to part-time work or lower-pressure jobs to carve out more time with their young children. But renewing careers that have been on hiatus is not easy, and women will always suffer

vocationally if it is they who must take off to nurture children. There is, obviously, another way: fathers can accept more home and family responsibilities, even to the point of interrupting their own careers. "I expect a significant change by 2020," says sociologist Hochschild. "A majority of men married to working wives will share equally in the responsibilities of home." Perhaps tradition will keep us from ever truly equalizing either child rearing or ironing—in fact, surveys on chore sharing don't hold much promise for the harried working mother. But we have moved a long way since the 1950s. And just because we haven't tried family equality yet doesn't mean we won't ever try it.

That's the magic for American families in the 21st century: we can try many things. As certainly as anything can be estimated, women are not going to turn their backs on education and careers, are not going to leave the work force for adult lives as full-time homemakers and mothers. And the nation's businesses will encourage their efforts, if only because they will need the skilled labor. Yet Americans will not turn their backs completely on the idealized family we remember fondly. Thus, we must create accommodations that are new, but reflect our heritage. Our families will continue to be different in the 21st century except in one way. They will give us sustenance and love as they always have.

16. **transcends ideology:** goes beyond the opinions of a single group of people
17. **coalition:** alliance
18. **think tank:** group that does research and problem-solving
19. **resonant:** echoing

"What Happened to the Family?" by Jerrold K. Footlick. From *Newsweek*, 1990 Winter/Spring Special Issue.

Are employers responsible for the happiness of their employees on and off the job? The following selection addresses the relationship between job satisfaction and happiness at home. As you read, consider how a job influences a person's quality of life.

JOB, LIFE QUALITY WORK TOGETHER

Corporate response to employees' needs for maternity leave, child care, flexible hours, job sharing, and family and medical leave is good management.

But it's not enough, according to Susan Lambert, assistant professor in the school of social service administration at the University of Chicago.

"Helping with off-the-job issues is only one prong of the work structure," said Lambert, who has a doctorate in social work and organizational psychology from the University of Michigan.

"What employers also have to look at is the other prong: how the quality of work affects the ability to handle your responsibilities at home. When you hate your job so much every day that you bring that feeling home, you don't have much left to offer your family.

"If you work for eight hours a day in a factory that's awful, where management is oppressive,[1] even if your employer offers child care, you still won't have psychological energy for your family."

The sociologist, whose thesis[2] is that family life affects work life and vice versa, believes that the "economic climate is ripe for changes in the

---

1. **oppressive:** overly harsh or strict
2. **thesis:** position set forth for discussion

corporate culture" because of the projected shortage in the 1990s of qualified personnel.

"Businesses have to get rid of the male model of running a company, the 1950s' approach, and instead manage for diversity," she said. "The workplace needs to be restructured in a very large sense, giving employees a bigger voice in how they do their job and what they do, keeping an ear to employees' needs."

That employers might be responsible for the happiness of their employees is a relatively new concept. In the "olden" days, the prevalent[3] attitude was if you didn't like your job, tough. And if you had family problems, they weren't the employer's responsibility.

Today, changes in corporate attitudes toward job and family issues are "essential to make the workplace work," says June Baldino Siegler of the American Management Association in New York.

"Absolute bliss is to have a good job and a supportive manager—and at the same time to be free of worry about child care," said Siegler, a human resource management authority. "If your job exhausts you and you're unmotivated because of deficiencies in the workplace, you will go home depressed and depleted.

"The role of management is to avoid this, to get the job done, and to make the

---

3. **prevalent:** widely accepted

organization successful. It's important to keep employees motivated and happy."

Siegler says that "as more and more professional managers with backgrounds in theories that motivate people and in organizational behavior move into the workplace, the better it will be."

She also sees the influx of women into management as a positive step, because "female managers tend to do better on relationships and may be more supportive."

Sociologist Lambert says the issues are becoming clearer, because "the boundaries between work and home are a lot less distinct. We know that when there's a crisis at home or at work, each is affected. Work and family interact with each other in a subtle way. It doesn't make sense to study one without the other."

And she has studied them together, completing research titled "The ecology[4] of work and home: The inter-relationship between employment and family." It was published in the *Journal of Organizational Behavior* in 1991.

"I wanted to look at not only how family affects work attitudes and behavior, but also at how work affects family attitudes and behavior," she said. "I take an ecological approach, which means instead of looking in one sphere and focusing only on work, I also studied how much your spouse earns and how many children you have, factors that make a difference on the job."

Earlier work on the subject made her aware that statistical literature only included men. "Part of my work is to extend theories of job structures to include women and their lives off the job," Lambert said.

She studied 605 men and 225 women in a standard sampling of the U.S. work force compiled by the Institute for Social Research at the University of Michigan.

"For women, it's a pretty complex texture," Lambert said. "One of the major things I found is that women suffer when they don't have meaningful work, when it's stressful or not a rewarding part of their lives. Jobs are still structured for the man who has a woman at home taking care of his personal responsibilities. Women pay a big price for that."

She points out that "women in low-status, low-paying jobs need the most help on the job and are getting the least."

The much-welcomed family benefits, Lambert notes, "are, in some cases, implemented as a pacifier, instead of making major structural changes that would make a difference in people's lives. In some ways, it's easier to provide child care than to give people more input into the decision-making process."

---

4. ecology: study of the relationships between people and their environments

---

"Job, Life Quality Work Together," by Susan Kleiman. From the *Chicago Tribune*, December 8, 1989.

Is laughter good medicine? Read to discover ways humor can help people cope with life's problems.

Getting More Smileage out of Your Life

Humor is no longer just a laughing matter. In fact, it is the easiest, cheapest, and most enjoyable way to alleviate stress. In a world with ever-increasing time pressures and demands, it is more important than ever to be able to manage stress effectively. Wearing a thick skin and developing the ability to laugh at life are skills that can provide considerable relief from tension, anxiety, anger, and other emotional pain.

Science Bears out Laughter's Benefits

Scientific research has confirmed that laughter is indeed important to health and has significant therapeutic[1] benefits. Perhaps the most well-known story is that of Norman Cousins. In his book, *Anatomy of an Illness,* he reported that daily doses of laughter resulted in apparent changes in his blood chemistry,

---

1. **therapeutic:** healing or preserving health

which assisted in his recovery from a degenerative[2] spinal disease. Studies substantiate[3] that laughter can relieve pain, apparently through the release of endorphins, the body's natural pain-killers, into the blood stream. By "treating" himself with laughter, Cousins may have been doing naturally what medication does chemically—relieving pain and promoting healing.

Humor as Stress Healer

Humor also seems to provide some protection against the effects of negative emotions. Its cathartic[4] effects help people generally feel better and more relaxed after laughing. Laughter produces a sense of well-being that helps create a positive outlook on life. People with a good sense of humor are generally more flexible and can cope better with stress. In addition, the positive feelings that laughter helps generate can create an atmosphere that enhances healing.

Take a look at the tips listed here for ways to refuel the humor in your life. And remember that laughter really can be "the best medicine."

---

2. **degenerative:** growing worse in structure or function
3. **substantiate:** confirm
4. **cathartic:** relieving emotional tensions

The following tips are geared to help you get more *"Smileage"* out of your life:

✳ Imitate and practice mannerisms of your favorite comedian. Under stress ask, "How would _____ handle this?" What can you imitate or borrow from this person's approach to life?

✳ Pretend you're on "Candid Camera." Distance yourself from a stressful situation for a few minutes, look around, and notice all the silly human activities that seemed so serious a few minutes ago.

✳ Try humor meditation. During the most tense part of your day, read a funny joke from a book or listen to a tape of your favorite comedian.

✳ Cultivate five-year-old children as friends.

✳ Celebrate Halloween monthly.

✳ Remember the two most important rules of stress management:
    1. Don't sweat the small stuff.
    2. It's all small stuff.

"Getting More Smileage out of Your Life," by Leslie Gerson. From *A Lifetime of Health*, July/August 1989.

Should school-aged children be left alone at home while parents work?
This is a hard question for many parents, and the opinions of child care
professionals vary widely. Read to learn about some important issues to
consider when deciding if self care can be a suitable option.

Sobel/Klonsky/The Image Bank

How Do Kids Really Feel about Being Home Alone?

When the First National Conference on Latchkey Children convened in Boston in May 1984, it immediately became clear that the subject of children in self care polarizes[1] people. In a session dealing with research on the topic, one panelist stressed the fear and safety risks school-age children face when they are taking care of themselves during the out-of-school hours. A second researcher, whose survey had just been published in a popular parents' magazine, argued that we simply do not know whether being a latchkey child has negative consequences.

Incensed with his viewpoint, the audience hardly gave him a chance to present his case.

When we ask, "How do kids really feel about being home alone?" we get different answers depending to a great extent on who gives the answer and where it is reported. Many child care professionals believe that self care brings with it a number of risks and should not be taken for granted as an adequate child care solution for school-age children. However, popular magazines and newspapers

1. **polarizes:** divides into opposing groups

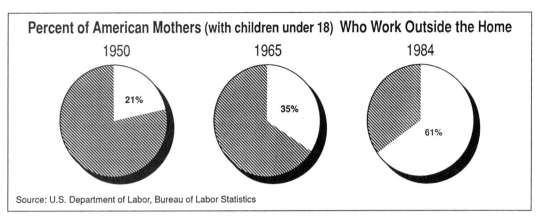

Percent of American Mothers (with children under 18) Who Work Outside the Home

1950 — 21%

1965 — 35%

1984 — 61%

Source: U.S. Department of Labor, Bureau of Labor Statistics

that target a working mother audience favor the view that self care is safe and quite manageable if children are prepared with the necessary skills to protect, discipline, and entertain themselves.

What is it about this subject that generates such controversy? Perhaps it is the realization that there is so much at stake for parents. Working parents are being forced to choose between perhaps their two highest priorities: working (in many cases for financial survival, not for professional fulfillment) and adequate child care. Many of these parents would not have chosen self care if given an option. Since it was the only available solution, emotions about the situation run high.

The practice of leaving children in self care is widespread in every community. Currently, well over half of all mothers with children under 18 years of age and 54 percent of mothers with children under six are in the work force. This is in marked contrast to 1940, when under nine percent of mothers with minor children were employed, and even after World War II, when just twice that many mothers of minor children were working. As a result of this shift, the majority of America's children are growing up in situations where either both parents or the sole parent is employed outside the home.

It has become increasingly difficult to provide supervision for school-age children when community institutions established for this purpose have not kept pace with the changing structure of the family. While recent census data suggest that only 7.2 percent of children between the ages of five and 13—about two million children—spend time in self care, a number of other sources estimate that over a quarter of the children between six and 14 years old spend time in self care, most of them regularly. (There are several plausible explanations why census figures would be artificially low. Among them are guilt on the part of the responding parent for leaving the child alone, and a hesitancy, stemming from safety concerns, to reveal that the child is sometimes left unsupervised.)

Research on the impact of self care is mixed. Some studies support the practice. Hyman Rodman and his associates at the University of North Carolina compared 4th graders in adult care with 4th graders in self care on measures of self-esteem,[2] sense of control over their own lives, and social skills. They found no difference in feelings between children in self care and those supervised by parents. In their study of 1,200 children in kindergarten through 8th grade, Diane Hedin and her colleagues at the University of Minnesota had similar findings. When asked how they felt about being in self care, 80 percent of the children in self care said that they loved it or liked it. It is interesting to note that both of these studies were cited in popular magazines that write for a working mother audience. While Deborah Vandell of the University of Texas automatically assumed that going home to a latchkey situation would prove to be bad for children, her study showed that there were no differences in parents', peers' or the children's own ratings of social and study skills between those who went home to their mothers and those in latchkey situations.

Other studies are not so optimistic about the impact of self care on school-age children. Laurence Steinberg of the University of Wisconsin questions Rodman's results on common sense grounds and in light of his own research on latchkey children. He states that the effects of self care are considerably more subtle than measurable loss of self-esteem or other sophisticated psychological constructs.[3] He points out that the public's concern about latchkey children revolves mainly around the fears and worries of these children, the dangers unsupervised children may be exposed to and their susceptibility to peer pressure, particularly when they

reach adolescence. His own studies indicate that the more removed from adult supervision adolescents are, the more susceptible they are to peer pressure to commit antisocial acts. This view is echoed by another researcher, Thomas Long, who found that as more children spend more time unattended in their own homes, the incidence of experimentation with alcohol and sex increases.

In a demonstration and research project conducted for the National Committee for Prevention of Child Abuse (NCPCA) and funded by the Head Start Bureau, ACYF (Administration for Children, Youth, and Families), we gained some new insights about how kids feel when they are home alone, in addition to testing a self-care preparation curriculum. The project, "Balancing Work and Family Life," tested an educational curriculum called "I'm in Charge," developed by the Kansas Committee for Prevention of Child Abuse for children in self care and their parents. The course—which was taught by trained volunteers from local NCPCA chapters in over 40 sites in eight states—teaches children and parents the skills necessary for safety and survival in self care settings. It does not promote or encourage self care, but rather assists families in deciding if self care is an appropriate option for them within their own unique environment.

The course consists of five sessions. Children attend all five sessions, while parents attend the first and last. In the first session, parents learn to evaluate

---

2. **self-esteem:** belief in oneself
3. **constructs:** theories

their child's ability to stay successfully in a self-care situation with a minimum of risk. They also discuss the benefits and risks of self care and explore alternative strategies and placements. Appropriate rule making and the importance of consistency[4] are emphasized, and parent and child are given tasks to complete together.

In session two, children describe the current rules in their homes, and they receive instruction in effective communication techniques that they can use with their parents when discussing their feelings about these rules. Personal safety skills regarding telephone calls, responding to strangers, and protection from sexual assault are reviewed and clarified. Reviews of existing educational prevention programs are also provided.

Session three focuses on discrimination between emergency and non-emergency situations. Children practice using the 911 emergency number and review procedures that they can use in non-emergency situations. They also learn a problem-solving strategy that they use later in the course and complete a homework assignment to identify fire escape routes and potential home safety hazards.

The fourth session examines the serious responsibility assumed by children caring for brothers and sisters and other children. Participants apply the problem-solving strategy that was introduced in the third session to devise realistic solutions for a variety of common problem situations. Three different models of division of power are discussed and children identify the

Elyse Lewin/The Image Bank

model used in their homes. The children also receive instruction in basic child care techniques, again emphasizing the importance of clear and continuing communication.

Parents and children attend the last session together and raise any concerns or questions they may have about material covered in previous meetings. Each family develops its own contract for self (or supervised) child care and the house rules are committed to paper for future use.

From this project—conducted with more than 1,000 children and 600 parents—we learned that it is possible to communicate self care techniques to

4. consistency: always holding to the same practices

children between eight and 12 years old through methods suggested in the curriculum. As the course progressed, parents and their children talked more about what could happen when the child was home alone, and the children understood more clearly what their parents wanted them to do in these situations. Tangible[5] preparation gradually replaced the guilt or fear that had prevented acknowledging real, if unlikely, disasters when children are unsupervised by adults.

What are we to make of the differing study findings regarding the impact of self care on children? If we are realistic, we will acknowledge that some kids probably do quite well in self care, while others—especially the younger ones—will have problems with it. In either case, self care is an arrangement set up to meet the needs of working parents and not necessarily the needs of the child. The findings of this project accentuate the fact that for most children, self care is no substitute for adult-supervised child care.

---

5. tangible: actual; real

"How Do Kids Really Feel about Being Home Alone?" by Ellen Gray and Peter Coolsen. From *Children Today*, July–August 1987.

Resources for Finding Out about Care for School-age Children

• **Your local school district** The teachers and principal at your child's school may know about school-age child-care programs in your community. Many schools offer before- and after-school care.

• **Your employer** Some employers have programs to help employees find school-age child care.

• **The Yellow Pages of your telephone book** Check under *Child Care* or *Social and Human Services*.

• **Child care resource and referral agencies** These groups, also in the Yellow Pages, can provide lists of school-age child-care programs and family day-care homes (where someone cares for children in his or her home), guidelines on how to evaluate care, and other services.

• **Government agencies** The Licensing Division of your State Human or Social Services Department can tell where to find state-licensed programs in your area. Other agencies such as Parks and Recreation departments sometimes offer programs.

• **Local churches, community centers, and civic groups** Many organizations may sponsor or know about after-school programs. Such organizations may include the YMCA/YWCA, local library, Junior League, League of Women Voters, National Organization for Women, National Council of Jewish Women, or Salvation Army.

• **Friends, neighbors, or parents of your child's classmates** Such people can tell you about programs and about their own experiences with these programs.

• **Some other organizations to contact for information about child care** The following organizations can provide information about various child-care options, including self care.

Project Home Safe	Child Care Action Campaign	School-Age Child Care Project
1555 King Street	330 Seventh Avenue, 18th floor	Wellesley College
Alexandria, VA 22314	New York, NY 10001	Center for Research on Women
		Wellesley, MA 12181

Unit 5: Economics

*the study of how goods and
services are produced, distributed,
and consumed*

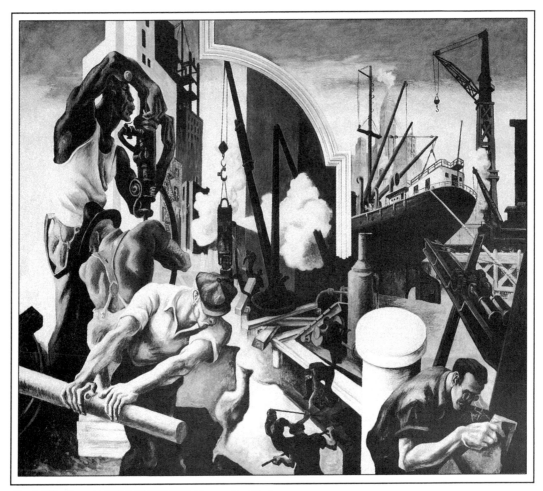

City Building from AMERICA TODAY, 1930, Thomas Hart Benton
Collection, The Equitable

Do you pay attention to daily news reports about the United States and world economies? Read the following selection for some basic knowledge of how economies work.

Economics

Most people want more than they can afford to buy. If a family buys one thing, they may not be able to afford something else they would like. The same is true of nations. Whether a nation is rich or poor, most of its people want more than they can afford. They seek better schools, more houses, and stronger armed forces. The field of economics studies how the things people need and want are made and brought to them. It also studies how people and nations choose the things they buy from among the many things they want.

Economists (specialists in economics) define *economics* as the study of how

goods and services get produced and how they are distributed. By *goods and services,* economists mean everything that can be bought and sold. By *produced,* they mean the processing and making of goods and services. By *distributed,* they mean the way goods and services are divided among people.

In all countries, the resources used to produce goods and services are *scarce.* That is, no nation has enough farms, factories, or workers to produce everything that everyone would like. Money is also scarce. Few people have enough money to buy everything they want when they want it. Therefore, people everywhere must choose the best possible way to use their resources and money. Children may have to choose whether to spend their allowance on a motion picture or a hamburger. Storekeepers may have to choose whether to take a summer vacation or to use their savings to buy more merchandise. A nation may have to choose whether to use tax money to build more highways or more submarines. In economic terms, the children, the storekeepers, and the nation all must *economize* in order to satisfy their most important needs and wants. This means they must try to use the resources they have to produce the things they most want.

Economic Problems

Every nation must organize the production and distribution of goods and services wanted by its citizens. To do this, a nation's economic system must solve four basic problems: (1) What shall be produced? (2) How shall goods and services be produced? (3) Who shall get the goods and services? and (4) How fast shall the economy grow?

What shall be produced? No nation can produce enough goods and services to satisfy all its people. But which goods and services are most important? Should land be used to raise corn or wheat? Should factories be used to produce rockets or television sets?

How shall goods and services be produced? Should each family raise its own food and make its own clothing? Or should special industries be developed to provide these products? Should many workers be used in an industry? Or

should more machines be built to do various jobs?

Who shall get the goods and services? Should everyone have an equal share of goods and services? Which goods and services should go only to people who can afford to buy them? Which goods and services should be distributed in some other way?

How fast shall the economy grow? An economy grows when it produces more goods and services. A nation must decide what proportion of its scarce resources should be used to build factories and machines and provide more education for its young people, all of which will increase future production. How much of a nation's resources should be used to produce goods and services, such as food and clothing, for immediate use? In addition, the nation must decide how to avoid unemployment and other economic setbacks that waste resources.

How the Economy Grows

An economy must grow to provide people with an increasing *standard of living*—that is, more and better goods and services. In general, the faster a country's economy grows, the faster its standard of living rises.

Making the economy grow. Four main elements make it possible for nations to produce goods and services. These elements, called *productive resources,* are: (1) natural resources, (2) capital, (3) a labor force, and (4) technology. Economists define *natural resources* as all land and raw materials, such as minerals, water, and sunlight. *Capital* includes factories, tools, supplies, and equipment. The word *capital* also means

Gross National Products of Nations in 1987

Country	Billions of dollars	Country	Billions of dollars
Brazil	291.3	Mexico	139.2
Canada	402.1	Nepal	2.8
China, Mainland	470.7	Nigeria	23.3
Colombia	33.9	North Korea	25.9
Egypt	71.2	Philippines	34.6
Ethiopia	5.2	Soviet Union	2,460.0
France	868.3	South Africa	77.1
India	246.0	South Korea	118.0
Iran	257.8	Switzerland	179.4
Iraq	56.5	Thailand	45.1
Italy	746.4	United Kingdom	667.0
Japan	2,369.0	United States	4,527.0
Kenya	7.6	Yugoslavia	60.5

Source: U.S. Arms Control and Disarmament Agency, *World Military Expenditures and Arms Transfers,* annual. Data from International Bank for Reconstruction and Development and U.S. Central Intelligence Agency.

the money that can be used to buy these things. *Labor force* means all people who work or are seeking work, and their education and skills. *Technology* refers to scientific and business research and inventions.

In order to grow, a nation's economy must add to its productive resources. For example, a nation must use some of its resources to build factories, heavy equipment, and other *capital goods.* Then these capital goods can help produce more goods in the future. A nation also must locate and develop additional natural resources, create new technologies, and train scientists, workers, and business managers, who will direct future production. The knowledge of these people is known as *human capital.*

Measuring economic growth. The value of all goods and services produced in any year makes up a nation's *gross national product.* An economy's rate of

growth is measured by the change in its gross national product over a period of years. The U.S. gross national product, when adjusted for inflation, has increased at an average rate of about three percent each year for the past hundred years.

Another way of measuring a nation's economic growth is to study the standard of living of its people. To judge standard of living, economists sometimes divide a nation's total gross national product by its entire population. The resulting figure is called the *per capita GNP.* In 1985, the per capita GNP of the United States was $16,400—that is, if all the goods and services produced in the United States that year were divided evenly among all the people, each person would receive about $16,400 worth. About three-fourths of the world's people live in developing countries, which taken together had a per capita GNP of $570 in 1985.

Kinds of Economic Systems

Different economic systems have developed because nations have never agreed on how to solve their basic economic problems. Three important economic systems today are (1) capitalism, (2) mixed economies, and (3) Communism. The economies of many countries include elements from several different economic systems.

Capitalism is the economic system of the United States, Canada, and many other countries throughout the world. It is called *capitalism* because an individual can own land and such *capital* as factories, apartment buildings, and railroads. Capitalism is also known as *free enterprise* because it allows people to carry out their economic activities largely free from government control.

The Scottish economist Adam Smith first stated the principles of the capitalist system in the 1700s. Smith believed that governments should not interfere in most business affairs. He said the desire of business people to earn a profit, when regulated by competition, would work almost like an "invisible hand" to produce what consumers want. Smith's philosophy is known as *laissez faire* (noninterference).

Adam Smith's emphasis on individual economic freedom still forms the basis of capitalism. But the growth and complexity of modern businesses, cities, and technologies have led the American people to give the government more economic duties than Smith gave it. In fact, many economists call the American system *modified free enterprise* because the government plays such an important part in it.

Mixed economies involve more government control and planning than do capitalist economies. In a mixed economy, the government owns and runs such important industries as steel mills, coal mines, and railroads. Most other industries may be privately owned. *Socialism* is the main type of mixed economy.

Some nations with mixed economies are democracies, including Great Britain and Sweden. The people of these nations elect the government and vote on some economic policies. They also may vote to increase or reduce the amount of control the government has over the economy. The economic system of such nations is often called *democratic socialism*.

Communism is based on government ownership of nearly all productive resources. In a Communist country, the government directs all important economic activity. It decides what shall be produced and in what quantity. It sets wages and prices. It also plans the rate of economic growth. Consumers can spend their money largely as they wish. But their choice of goods is limited to what the government makes available. Under Communism, people have little control over the government's policies. Members of the Communist Party make major decisions. China is an example of a Communist country.

The Water Is Wide

What would you do if you lived in a community where the only industry offering work was lost? Read to discover what happened to one community when pollution destroyed the people's means for earning a living.

Yamacraw is an island off the South Carolina mainland not far from Savannah, Georgia. The island is fringed with the green, undulating marshes of the southern coast; shrimp boats ply the waters around her and fishermen cast their lines along her bountiful shores. Deer cut through her forests in small silent herds. The great southern oaks stand broodingly on her banks. The island and the waters around her teem with life. There is something eternal and indestructible about the tide-eroded shores and the dark, threatening silences of the swamps in the heart of the island. Yamacraw is beautiful because man has not yet had time to destroy this beauty.

The twentieth century has basically ignored the presence of Yamacraw. The island is populated with black people who depend on the sea and their small farms for a living. Several white families live on the island in a paternalistic,[1] but in many ways symbiotic,[2] relationship with

---

1. **paternalistic:** fatherly
2. **symbiotic:** dependent on each other

their neighbors. Only one white family actively participates in island life to any perceptible degree. The other three couples have come to the island to enjoy their retirement in the obscurity of the island's remotest corners. Thus far, no bridge connects the island with the mainland, and anyone who sets foot on the island comes by water. The roads of the island are unpaved and rutted by the passage of ox carts, still a major form of transportation. The hand pump serves up questionable water to the black residents who live in their small familiar houses. Sears, Roebuck catalogues perform their classic function in the crudely built privies,[3] which sit, half-hidden, in the tall grasses behind the shacks. Electricity came to the island several years ago. There is something unquestionably moving about the line of utility poles coming across the marsh, moving perhaps because electricity is a bringer of miracles and the journey of the faceless utility poles is such a long one—and such a humane one. But there are no telephone poles (electricity is enough of a miracle for one century). To call the island you must go to the Beaufort Sheriff's Office and talk to the man who works the radio. Otherwise, Yamacraw remains aloof and apart from the world beyond the river.

It is not a large island, nor an important one, but it represents an era and a segment of history that is rapidly dying in America. The people of the island have changed very little since the Emancipation Proclamation.[4] Indeed, many of them have never heard of this proclamation. They love their island with genuine affection but have watched the young people move to the city, to the lands far away and far removed from Yamacraw. The island is dying, and the people know it.

In the parable[5] of Yamacraw there was a time when the black people supported themselves well, worked hard, and lived up to the sacred tenets[6] laid down in the Protestant ethic.[7] Each morning the strong young

---

3. **privies:** outhouses
4. **Emancipation Proclamation:** declaration that freed the slaves in1863
5. **parable:** story that offers a moral lesson
6. **tenets:** beliefs
7. **Protestant ethic:** belief in the importance of hard work and thrifty living

men would take to their bateaux[8] and search the shores and inlets for the large clusters of oysters, which the women and old men in the factory shucked into large jars. Yamacraw oysters were world famous. An island legend claims that a czar of Russia once ordered Yamacraw oysters for an imperial banquet. The white people propagate[9] this rumor. The blacks, for the most part, would not know a czar from a fiddler crab, but the oysters were good, and the oyster factories operating on the island provided a substantial living for all the people. Everyone worked and everyone made money. Then a villain appeared. It was an industrial factory situated on a knoll above the Savannah River many miles away from Yamacraw. The villain spewed its excrement[10] into the river, infected the creeks, and as silently as the pull of the tides, the filth crept to the shores of Yamacraw. As every good health inspector knows, the unfortunate consumer who lets an infected oyster slide down his throat is flirting with hepatitis.[11] Someone took samples of the water around Yamacraw, analyzed them under a microscope, and reported the results to the proper officials. Soon after this, little white signs were placed by the oyster banks forbidding anyone to gather the oysters. Ten thousand oysters were now as worthless as grains of sand. No czar would order Yamacraw oysters again. The muddy creatures that had provided the people of the island with a way to keep their families alive were placed under permanent quarantine.[12]

Since a factory is soulless and faceless, it could not be moved to understand the destruction its coming had wrought. When the oysters became contaminated, the island's only industry folded almost immediately. The great migration began. A steady flow of people faced with starvation moved toward the cities. They left in search of jobs. Few cities had any intemperate demand for professional oyster-shuckers, but the people were somehow assimilated.[13] The population of the island diminished considerably. Houses surrendered their tenants to the city and signs of sudden departure were rife in the interiors of deserted homes. Over 300 people left the island. They left reluctantly, but left permanently and returned only on sporadic visits to pay homage to the relatives too old or too stubborn to leave. As the oysters died, so did the people.

---

8. **bateaux:** light-weight, flat-bottomed boats
9. **propagate:** spread
10. **excrement:** waste matter
11. **hepatitis:** liver disease that easily spreads from person to person
12. **quarantine:** restriction that keeps something isolated so it cannot spread disease
13. **assimilated:** absorbed into the main culture

From *The Water Is Wide*, by Pat Conroy.

Are you preparing for the job market of the year 2000? The following selection presents information about the changing job market and the levels of education the market demands of its labor force. As you read the selection and study the chart provided, consider your career goal and how you can achieve it.

Labor Force Projections
for the
Year 2000

Did you know that the United States labor force will look very different in the year 2000 than it did the decade or so before then?

Younger workers will become a smaller part of the labor force. The share of workers 16 to 24 years old will decline because the size of the age group is shrinking. This group made up 19 percent of the labor force in 1988, but its share will fall to 16 percent by the year 2000.

The number of workers between 25 and 54 years of age will increase. This group, which includes the large baby-boom generation, made up 69 percent of the total labor force in 1988 and will make up 72 percent in the year 2000.

Though the number of workers 55 and older will rise, the proportion of the labor force composed of workers in this age group will remain steady at 12 percent.

Women will continue to increase their presence in the labor force. Their share of the labor force will increase from 45 percent in 1988 to 47 percent in 2000.

The portion of whites in the labor force will decrease from approximately 86 percent in 1988 to 84 percent in 2000. Over this same period, the portion of African-Americans will rise from 11 percent to 12 percent, and the portion of Asians and others will increase from three percent to four percent.

The Hispanic labor force will grow very rapidly. It will have risen from eight million in 1988 to 14 million in 2000. As a result, the Hispanic share of the labor force will increase from seven percent to 10 percent. Immigration and a rise in the native-born Hispanic population will stimulate this growth.

Driven by a growing demand for services, the service-producing sector will provide 16.6 million new jobs. The service-producing sector includes education, hospitals, retail trade, government, finance, insurance, real estate, wholesale trade, transportation, communications, and utilities. In the year 2000, 77.8 percent of all jobs will be in these areas.

Health and business services will account for about a third of total job growth from 1988 to 2000. Among the fastest-growing of all industries are outpatient care facilities, physicians' offices, medical and dental laboratories, computer and data processing services, and personnel supply services.

Retail trade will provide more than 3.7 million new jobs and will account for 22 percent of total job growth. Eating and drinking places will add more jobs than any other single industry.

The growth of the goods-producing sector will be small compared to that of the service-producing sector. The goods-producing sector, which includes manufacturing, construction, agriculture, forestry, fishing, and mining, will add only half a million new jobs between 1988 and 2000. The number of jobs available in manufacturing and mining will be lower in 2000 than in 1988.

Seven of the 10 fastest-growing occupations involve health services. These occupations include medical assistant, home health aide, radiologic technician, medical records technician, medical secretary, physical therapist, and surgical technologist. Also among the 10 fastest-growing occupations are paralegal, data processing equipment repairer, and operations research analyst.

The following 20 occupations are large and, while not experiencing the fastest growth, they will grow the most in the numbers of people employed. These occupations together will provide 40 percent of all new jobs: retail salesperson; registered nurse; janitor and cleaner; waiter and waitress; general manager and top executive; general office clerk; secretary; nursing aide and orderly; truckdriver; receptionist and information clerk; cashier; guard; computer programmer; food counter worker; food preparation worker; licensed practical nurse; secondary school teacher; computer systems analyst; accountant and auditor; and kindergarten and elementary school teacher.

The projected growth of the broad occupational groups shows the increasing need for more education. Occupations in which a large proportion of workers have college degrees are among the fastest growing. Occupations in which a large proportion of workers have less than four years of high school are generally among the slowest growing. Workers with more education also earn more and are less likely to be unemployed.

From *Occupational Outlook Quarterly,* Fall 1989, published by the U.S. Department of Labor, Bureau of Labor Statistics.

The Growing Need for Education

Several major groups of occupations are growing faster than average. Workers in the fastest-growing major occupational groups have the highest educational attainment and the highest earnings.

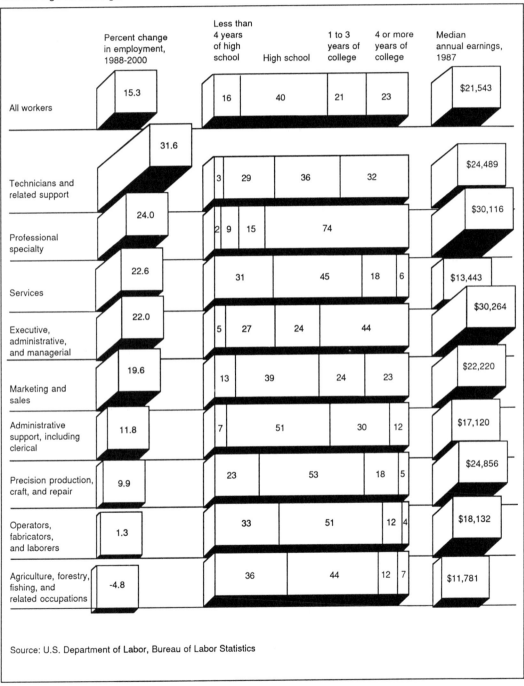

Occupation	Percent change in employment, 1988-2000	Less than 4 years of high school	High school	1 to 3 years of college	4 or more years of college	Median annual earnings, 1987
All workers	15.3	16	40	21	23	$21,543
Technicians and related support	31.6	3	29	36	32	$24,489
Professional specialty	24.0	2	9	15	74	$30,116
Services	22.6	31	45	18	6	$13,443
Executive, administrative, and managerial	22.0	5	27	24	44	$30,264
Marketing and sales	19.6	13	39	24	23	$22,220
Administrative support, including clerical	11.8	7	51	30	12	$17,120
Precision production, craft, and repair	9.9	23	53	18	5	$24,856
Operators, fabricators, and laborers	1.3	33	51	12	4	$18,132
Agriculture, forestry, fishing, and related occupations	-4.8	36	44	12	7	$11,781

Source: U.S. Department of Labor, Bureau of Labor Statistics

In what ways can job seekers benefit from a labor shortage? Some people believe the predicted labor shortage in the United States will mean better job opportunities for minorities. Read to discover why William Raspberry, a noted African-American columnist, believes minorities will not benefit unless they prepare for challenges ahead.

Minorities Won't Automatically Gain from Labor Shortage

Some optimists who ought to know better are taking comfort in the demographic[1] projections of an aging American work force and a labor-short economy.

By the year 2000, we are told, some three quarters of the new workers will be minorities and women. Black, brown, and female workers will be in such demand that not even America's deeply ingrained racism and sexism can prevent their progress.

I have no confidence in projections because I think the optimism is based on false premises.[2]

What do the numbers mean? Well, two things. To employers, they mean the necessity of learning to deal with diversity. To be successful in a labor-short future will require businesses to develop as big an employee pool as they can, and also to create a work environment capable of getting out of all of our people the talent they have to offer.

And what is the meaning for the minorities? The temptation is to look at the projections as virtual guarantees of

---

1. **demographic:** dealing with the characteristics of the population
2. **premises:** reasons for drawing conclusions

employment opportunity, even for the marginally[3] qualified.

It's a pleasant thought. But it might be prudent[4] to entertain a more sobering one: If America's manufacturers and producers of products can't find enough workers to remain competitive, the first response will be to import the necessary workers.

The next likely response will be to export the jobs.

Both things, in fact, are already happening. In the past decade, the American electronics industry, for example, has created more jobs in Asia than in America. The result is a loss of entry-level jobs that might have been available to undereducated minorities here. But since it also means a loss of jobs for skilled and educated Americans, there will be a near-irresistible political pressure to restrict the outflow of American industry.

But whence will come the political pressure to resist the influx of foreign workers? Not from the labor elite,[5] who will see the new immigrants as sources of new businesses and as new opportunities for themselves. Not from industry, which already is importing skilled workers at record rates.

The only pressure will come from America's hard-pressed minorities: typically too poorly educated and too unlikely to vote to make much difference.

Indeed, two respected social scientists—Ben Wattenberg and Karl Zinmeister of the American Enterprise Institute—have called for legislation to increase the flow of immigrants to America.

They propose a scheme that would benefit American industry and its educated classes, while penalizing only the undereducated minorities.

So what course does prudence demand? Clearly we will have to continue the push for diversity, pressing America, in its private associations and in the workplace, to reflect the contributions and the interests of all its citizens.

But we will also have to give a lot more attention to getting our people—especially our children—ready to take advantage of opportunity.

Too many of our children are behind from the day they enter kindergarten, because their parents have not imbued[6] them with what Dorothy Rich calls "megaskills"—the attitudes, habits, and intellectual stimulation necessary for school success. We have to teach people how to develop these skills: in high-school classrooms and in community-based parenting classes.

---

3. marginally: just barely
4. prudent: using sound judgement
5. elite: most powerful and privileged part of a group
6. imbued: influenced or spread through

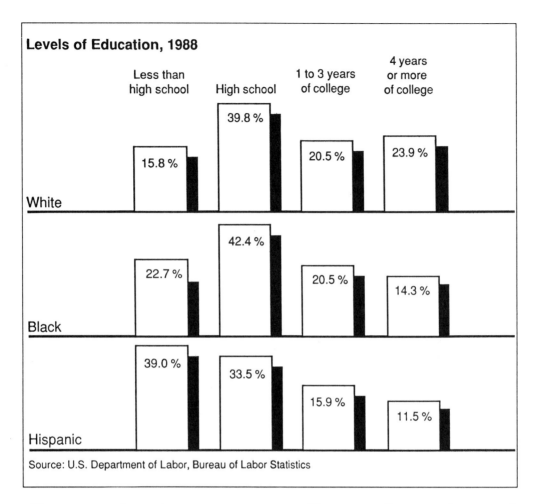

Levels of Education, 1988

White
- Less than high school: 15.8 %
- High school: 39.8 %
- 1 to 3 years of college: 20.5 %
- 4 years or more of college: 23.9 %

Black
- Less than high school: 22.7 %
- High school: 42.4 %
- 1 to 3 years of college: 20.5 %
- 4 years or more of college: 14.3 %

Hispanic
- Less than high school: 39.0 %
- High school: 33.5 %
- 1 to 3 years of college: 15.9 %
- 4 years or more of college: 11.5 %

Source: U.S. Department of Labor, Bureau of Labor Statistics

Too many of our teenagers are leaving school as dropouts, not merely because they are cheated of opportunity but also because they do not understand the extent to which their future is in their own hands.

Too many of our students fail to acquire fluency in English because we have not taught them that it can open more doors than even a college degree, and that poor English can close doors.

Too many of our people use racism as an excuse for not trying. We have to spread the word that racism, unfair though it may be, need not stand in the way of their success.

The demographic projections represent unprecedented opportunity for America's disadvantaged minorities. But opportunity isn't enough. Unless we can teach them the necessity of preparation and application, the year 2000 will find them on the outside looking in.